GW00546535

JOSEPH TOMELTY
A PORTRAIT

JOSEPH TOMELTY
A Portrait

SEAN M^CMAHON

Sean McMahon (signature)

LAGAN PRESS
BELFAST
2011

Published by
Lagan Press
Unit 45
Westlink Enterprise Centre
30-50 Distillery Street
Belfast BT12 5BJ
e-mail: lagan-press@e-books.org.uk
web: lagan-press.org.uk

© Sean McMahon, 2011

The moral rights of the author(s) have been asserted.

ISBN: 978 1 908188 17 5 (hbk)
978 1 908188 18 2 (pbk)
Author: McMahon, Sean
Title: Joseph Tomelty
A Portrait
2011

for Roma and Frances, without whose help ...

CONTENTS

Acknowledgements

My thanks are due to Maeve Breslin; Frank D'Arcy; Andrea Gorman; Joanna Harvey; Sophia Hillan; Anne Langford; Brian McMahon; Niamh McNamara, BBC Archivist; Andrea Dorman, Research Officer, Community Archive, Cultra; Paddy O'Carolan; Damian Smyth; the staff of the Linen Hall Library, especially the librarian, John Killen, Monica Cash, Ross Moore and Deborah Douglas; the staff of the Central Library, Derry, especially Jane Nicholas; and, primarily and superbly, Roma and Frances Tomelty.

Prologue

ONE DAY WHEN FRANCES TOMELTY, JOE Tomelty's second daughter, was travelling down the Falls Road in a trolleybus from her home in Belfast's Stockman's Lane, it stopped briefly out of respect to let a funeral pass by. It was on its way to Milltown Cemetery and, as was the custom of the time, there were many lines of walking mourners. She was young enough to be slightly embarrassed to see her father in the front row with a broad smile on his face while all about him were roaring with laughter at his stream of jokes. It was typical of the man that he believed a funeral should be a celebration of a life and with the obvious exception of a premature decease, not an unhappy occasion. It was also typical of the man who, never having quite recovered from a dreadful brain injury, still found the strength and the will to live his residual life to the full.

As Frances later realised, the same scene could have happened on the Shankill Road in a procession to the City Cemetery or on the way to Roselawn. Tomelty recognised no sectarian barriers and was greeted with equal enthusiasm in any part of the troubled city. At the height of his fame in the mid-1950s when he appeared regularly in films (eight in 1954 alone), on stage, on television and, spectacularly, on radio with his own intensely popular family 'soap', *The McCooeys*, though the term was not in use then, he was one of the most recognisable people in town. With his shock of white hair and kindly face (that could register great pathos and anger when required) he was used to being greeted by many friends and an even greater number of strangers seeking the briefest acquaintance.

Few outside Ireland realised that the actor who played the 'old codger' was only forty-one in 1952 and that by then he had written twelve plays, all excellent of their kind, three of them superb, and one a work of theatre equal to the best of any other twentieth-century dramatist; two novels, one set in his native town of Portaferry, the other in his adoptive city of Belfast, and 800,000 words of scripts for the most popular radio programme ever broadcast by BBC Northern Ireland. This prodigious output all but ceased in April 1955, and for forty more years he lived, conscious of his disability, but grateful, as he once put it, for what he had and for what he had lost. Until that visitation he looked set to become one of Ulster's all-round literary giants; even by the standard of the work already achieved he must be judged as a leading Irish writer and multi-talented man of the theatre. Now, in the year of the centenary of his birth, it is appropriate that to accompany the publication of a complete assembly of his plays, some account of his life should be written.

The chapters are generally in chronological order but because each deals with a different topic and may be read independently, there is some slight but necessary repetition.

1
Portaferry

IN THE COUNTY DOWN DIRECTORY FOR 1886, the anonymous compiler insisted: 'Portaferry deserves to be classed among the most charmingly picturesque places in Ireland' and goes on to advise that it is 'communicated with by means of a ferry from the village of Strangford on the western side'. Its population then, according to the 1881 census, was 1,674. The ferry which runs every thirty minutes the three-quarters of a mile NNW to Portaferry is still an essential lifeline for local fishermen and yachtsmen and in 2001 the town had 2,467 inhabitants. The long talon-like finger of the Ards Peninsula almost closes off Strangford Lough's access to the Irish Sea, nearly making it an inland sea. The Vikings, who appreciated a good anchorage when they saw one, called it 'fierce fjord', all too aware of the tidal race at the straits through which an estimated four hundred million tons of water charge twice a day.

The Tomelty family are native stock, the name being the earliest recorded in the local parish record. A charter granted in 1694 in the reign of William III (1689–1702) gave one Piers

Tomalty (sic) the right to run the ferry to Strangford. Joseph Tomelty was born on 5 March 1911, the firstborn of the seven children of James Tomelty and Mary Drumgoole, the daughter of a gamekeeper from Coolderry House, near Carrickmacross, County Monaghan, home of William Claude Brabazon Brownlow JP (1850–1914). There was music also on his mother's side; her father was known to doze at the fire, whistling in his sleep. Today the Drumgoole cousins have a dance band and write local songs – one is a music teacher. His father was known as Rollickin' James because of his ability with the fiddle, and few local dances at the crossroads lacked his contribution. He was a painter who had worked on the *Titanic* which he remembered was a 'three-coat job' so excellent was the finish on the doomed liner. Like many of his faith he was hounded out of the shipyard at a time of intense sectarian confrontation.

It was a musical house full of instruments: cello, accordion, cornet, flute and piano, and hundreds of songs old and new were continually sung. Peter, the youngest child, became a professional singer. Unable to do much about all this music, the mother, probably distracted by near poverty and an abundance of children, had no time for books; like Tarry Flynn's mother from the same county, she felt that 'curse o' God rhyming' was a waste of time.

It is ironic that her firstborn, who as an adult would be famous for his literary endeavours, should have been denied this artistic fare. It may explain his later voracious reading and may have given him a professional interest in such rigidity of attitude that formed the nucleus of some of his bleak women characters. He did have one book – a school text of *The Deserted Village* by Oliver Goldsmith (1728–74), a paean to a lost kindness and against the beginnings of factory farming and the dereliction of responsibility by nouveau riche landlords. Tomelty later told his daughter Rosemary, always known as Roma, that he could find equivalents for its characters among the people of Portaferry. The second most famous of Goldsmith's portraits is the village schoolmaster:

> And still they gazed and still the wonder grew
> That one small head could carry all he knew.

It is rather more waspish than that of the village preacher (based upon Goldsmith's own father) and one can find evidence that Tomelty was not happy at school. Certainly his childhood stammer was exacerbated rather than helped by his own teacher and the teachers in his play *Idolatry at Innishargie* (1942) and his novel *The Apprentice* (1953), are unpleasant creatures. One source of reading matter was Andy McVeigh, the sacristan of the local church, who lent him books; and with such a respectable provenance, his mother could not object. Tomelty loved both Andy and Mary Jane, his wife, and they constituted a significant part of his real education.

He discovered early a talent for mimicry of Scots tourists and while doing the voices showed no trace of an impediment. He was also very conscious of the beauty of the place and though he fished in small dinghies in inshore waters, he had always a healthy regard for the moody sea. In a television interview with his friend Sam Hanna Bell, made in 1969, he recalled walking along the sea front:

> Schooners would come into Portaferry Quay. You would pass along and note lovely poetic names like *The Maid of Trostan, The Passing Cloud, The Moss Rose, La Belle Marie.*

He also told the story, often repeated, of his Uncle Patrick's hearing a voice crying: 'Save a life! Save a life!' The old man, who always dressed like a sailor in navy blue gansey and blue peaked cap and claimed he had seen the ghosts of sailors at Rock Angus, continued: 'Then I heard the gargle of death in his throat.' Tomelty told the viewers: 'I could see the drowning body, the water rushing down his throat. The word picture haunted me until I wrote *All Souls' Night* – it all went into *All Souls' Night.*' He also used it in an early radio play, *The Elopement* (1939).

His County Down boyhood lasted a mere twelve years as he

left school in Ballyphilip to become an apprentice painter like most of the males in his family. He moved to Belfast on a scholarship and though he did not often return except to take the children down most years at Easter – Roma learned to walk in the demesne – he realised that his future lay in Belfast. A number of visits after the accident were undertaken as therapy. Eugene and Peter, his brothers, were regular visitors to the city, the latter once, as a boy, running away from Portaferry and arriving at Iris Drive where Tomelty and his wife Lena were living. She promptly put him on the bus for home. Kathleen, his eldest sister (still alive), remembers Joe as being very clever and always reading. Some family stories of his boyhood recall that he was known for tireless exploring about the town and surroundings. He was fond of visiting an old graveyard at Ballytrostan with ruinous vaults that were of special interest. In one he found that bees had made a nest inside a skull and he and his companions used to poke stripped sally rods with a few catchment leaves to get the honey. It was an image with great appeal to a lad with a keen visual sense, a skull dripping honey. Whether true or not he would retell the story often at table to the disgust of his mother-in-law Min Milligan, who in her characteristically trenchant way would respond with: 'Dirty oul' beast! You've put me off honey for life.'

When, much later, Tomelty, Roma and Peter visited the graveyard to look for the vault, he had no memory of the honey skull but did recall a song that he and other boys used to chant. They called it 'Widdicombe' from the name on a grave and they used to sit on the wall nearby and sing: 'Wid-ye-come? Wid-ye-go, Willie?' When, years later, the family visited the place, he suddenly remembered the word, 'Widdicombe'. Coincidentally the family rented Widdicombe's house at Tara for a year in 1956 but the name meant nothing to him then. Recently the place has been cleaned up and the crumbling vaults covered with neatly-mown grass. You can still hear the hollow echo of them beneath your feet if you stamp loudly enough. Other, perhaps imperfectly remembered, boyhood incidents involve a dead tree he once climbed and, accidentally breaking a branch, discovered a nest of bats which squeaked as they were disturbed, while he fell down out of the tree. In a china cabinet in the Portaferry house there was displayed a set of cheap delft decorated with red roses edged with black that the lad won at a fair in a competition for eating onions. The family often wondered whether hunger was not the real reason for his taking part.

Even by the standards of the time it was a normal childhood with neither luxuries nor extreme hardship. It was certainly spartan and for some time after the accident a kind of instinctive frugality asserted itself. For a writer/actor/man of the theatre it was as good a boyhood as any other. He had the dramatic beauty of the lough, the picturesque setting of the town and occasional visits of fit-up drama companies that specialised in such popular melodramas as *East Lynne* and *The Murder in the Red Barn*. One such troupe of players, Dobell and Company, so entranced him that he suddenly realised that he would rather be an actor than prime minister of Britain. In an interview with John Boyd for BBC Northern Ireland, broadcast on 13 March 1970, he said with a chuckle that 'acting broke out in me'. The place taught him the ways of the sea, a necessary part of the local culture, and he could always read the mood of the lough. As he told Boyd, 'In other places they look to the sky; in Portaferry we study the sea.'

His local knowledge stayed with him in spite of years of city living; as we will discover, he loved local names of flora and fauna, relished the hints of a lost tradition and developed an artist's eye for visual representation. His term was 'word pictures'. He also achieved a linguist's ear for flavoursome turns of local speech that stood him in good stead for his plays and the dialogue of his novels. As he listed in the interview mentioned above, the names of the ships that fascinated him as a boy, *Moss Rose, Passing Cloud, Summer Breeze, La Belle Marie* and *Sea Witch*, it was clear that they still could conjure up images and stories crying out to be told, the last named especially potent and regarded with respect if not actual fear. One day a schooner docked and its name, *Charles Stewart Parnell*, fascinated him. He asked an old seaman, who had a permanent perch on the end of the pier, where the name came from. 'A decent man the English set a trap for and he fell into it.'

Sir Walter Scott once apostrophised Scotland as ' ... Caledonia, stern and wild/Meet nurse for a poetic child'. Tomelty's artistic nurse was Portaferry but as an artist he was still an apprentice and for the moment a different indenture beckoned.

2

St Peter's

THE BELFAST OF THE EARLY DECADES of the
Northern Ireland state was a byword for sectarianism.
From the time of the early instinctive decision on the
part of its industrial magnates to make the small, once radical,
port into the Manchester or Birmingham of Ireland until the city's
zenith as Linenopolis just before the Great War, the town's
population had kept pace with its industrial expansion. It rose
from 37,277 in 1821 to 386,947 in 1911 though the Catholic
population throughout those nine decades rarely rose above a
quarter of the total. Any metropolis will attract immigrants from
the country and smaller towns to the natural centre and even then
there was a tendency, especially in the Ulster counties east of the
Bann, to look for work in the shipyards, the linen mills, the
foundries and the rope works that made the red-brick second city
internationally much more famous than the less industrialised
capital, Dublin.

Among this influx was inevitably a proportion of Catholics but
a kind of wise reluctance kept the numbers down. The regularly

recurring, often murderous, violence against the minority, especially during the marching season, kept all but the desperate well away from the Lagan. An especially cataclysmic event like the Great Famine of the 1840s brought an increase of those seeking relief from the hunger and the typhus. Ulster, apart from Donegal and parts of western Monaghan and Cavan, was not the area most severely affected by the blight but those most vulnerable, the poor, a majority of whom were Catholic, were prepared to risk anything to survive. There was no formal prohibition, apart from the contemporary graffiti equivalent of 'Taigs Out!', and workers of the lowest unskilled level were needed to man the burgeoning factories and mills.

They settled in enclaves, especially in the basin, so to speak, of the Falls Road, with smaller pockets in the Short Strand, the Markets, Smithfield and Ardoyne. They were poor and politically null but with the help of some biological sports – rich Catholics – and the Church, they established a kind of inner community with a devotional, nationalist and even aesthetic culture, fed by its all-Ireland source. This social self-sufficiency remained as a kind of bafflement to the Unionist majority in the city and its people were viewed with general suspicion and seasonal fear. A series of episcopal leaders, Crolly, Denvir, Dorrian and Henry, gradually built up their identity and confidence, though the last named tended to favour the slowly growing Catholic bourgeois in opposition to the lay leader of the area, 'Wee Joe' Devlin (1871–1934), who was very much a man of the people.

One of the early Catholic philanthropists, Bernard Hughes (1808–1887), managed to cater for his co-religionists both physically and spiritually. His bakery had managed to produce a dense kind of bread that banished hunger very effectively during the Famine years and gave him a kind of oblique immortality. His name was still remembered in the twentieth century because of this famous bun that caused any person called Hughes to be nicknamed 'Bap' and for a not very complimentary rhyme popular with children:

Barney Hughes's bread
Sticks to your belly like lead;
It's no wonder you fart like thunder –
Barney Hughes's bread.

His spiritual contribution was his personal involvement in the building of the St Peter's Pro-Cathedral right in the heart of Catholic West Belfast, a region loosely described as the Lower Falls. It was sited in the section known as the Pound Loney that gave its name to the predominantly Catholic area in the riven town and ran from there up past the top of Barrack Street to what was later Divis Street. The word 'loney' is a form of the Scots word 'loanen', a lane between fields. The cathedral's opening in 1866 gave a great impulse to the Catholic identity and when in 1885 the twin spires were completed, it became one of the most recognisable of the many ecclesiastical edifices of the city.

This inner city grew as the enclosing conurbation increased. Its denizens worked out a kind of *modus vivendi* with their intermittently inimical neighbours dreading the July Orange demonstrations as in a much minor way *they* feared the equivalent celebrations of the Ancient Order of Hibernians (AOH) later in the summer and on the feast of the national apostle. With the Government of Ireland Act of 1921, this isolated nationalist community found itself not only in a kind of social and cultural exile but at the mercy of government-approved paramilitaries who were granted a minimal respectability as special constables. The result of a virtual anti-Catholic pogrom in which there were many deaths, the violence exacerbated by a continuing, effectively suicidal, campaign by the northern IRA, was an ever greater withdrawal into a defensive enclave that literally refused to recognise the government of the new Northern Ireland state. This acute sense of victimisation felt by all Ulster nationalists was intensified by the passing in 1922 of a (temporary) Special Powers Act by the Unionist government under the aegis of the flinty Minister of Home Affairs, Sir Richard Dawson Bates (1876–1949). This effectively removed Habeas Corpus and it was made permanent in 1933 long after the threat was over. It was said to be the envy of the apartheid leaders of white South Africa. Though used draconically against those 'rotten' Protestants who cared more for bread than Orange collarettes, its main targets were Catholics and nationalists, especially ones with IRA sympathies, as that much depleted movement carried on the sacred 'armed struggle'.

According to the 1926 census, 95,658 Catholics formed around 23 per cent of the total population of 415,161 and without even the hope of the amelioration of their second-class citizenship, they survived by devising an informal structure that coexisted with the surrounding wider urban settlement. Its moral and artistic centre was the Lower Falls, effectively the close quarters of St Peter's. The Church more or less benevolently provided what the city fathers withheld. There was a cathedral-centred choir that did not confine its repertoire to plainchant. There were other lay aspects to clergy-approved and -sponsored social events, sports, dancing and drama. Tomelty, the young apprentice painter, was out of his indentures in 1932 and, both in work and play, was heavily involved in these activities. He had lived in the area since he was twelve years of age and was aware of every nuance of circumspect behaviour and special antennae-quivering language that the citizens used to discover, for reassurance or concern, the religion and politics of new acquaintances. Finding out 'what foot they dig with', to use the typical Ulsterism coined to cover the need for litmus testing, was crucial at its lowest level out of courtesy and at the other extreme out of regard for safety.

This exclusiveness was mitigated to some extent among the middle classes where in the growing suburbs professional people of 'both sides of the house', to use the other sectarian phrase, were on terms of, at least, politeness. They had not gone to the same schools or supported the same football teams but they were likely to be fellow members of the same golf club and to chat over the garden wall about the state of the wisteria. Working-class Catholics were employed, especially in the mills and in the lesser-skilled jobs in the yards and factories, but they were not at ease with 'the other sort' and were likely to be victims of harassment and worse at times of inter-creed tension.

And, of course, a recurrent theme of romantic literature, of Montague and Capulet, Abie's Irish Rose, and 'love across the barricades' had its reality even here in darkest Belfast. The nineteenth-century Church had reluctantly tolerated 'mixed' marriages, as they were called, but with the promulgation of the *Ne Temere* decree by Pope St Pius X (1835–1914) in 1908, the rules were tightened and non-Catholic partners had to promise that any children must be brought up in the Catholic faith. The decree was a reaffirmation of long-standing church teaching but its effect in Ireland, especially in the North, was significant. It was seen by the Ulster majority as a further example of the growth of Catholic power and a demonstration of little charity towards Protestants.

Coming from a small town like Portaferry, with a population in his youth of less than 2,000, where sheer social necessity required a more promiscuous mingling of the two sects, Tomelty would probably have had a greater acquaintance with Protestants than his Belfast friends. There was, of course, that staple of Irish life, the Big House and a family, Nugent. Once on a film set the tea-boy approached him shyly, admitting that he was one of the Portaferry Nugents, and wondering if he could get Tomelty a cup of tea. The idea tickled him greatly: 'A Nugent waiting on a Tomelty! By George ... '

As with the radical town at the time of the founding of the Society of United Irishmen, small minorities posed no threat; Protestants had contributed to the building of the first Belfast Catholic church, St Mary's (1784), but a steady quarter of the population, whose loyalty could not be trusted and who were clearly priest-ridden with an alien set of devotions, was uncomfortably large. Tomelty, instinctually lacking the slightest trace of bigotry, neither feared nor disliked members of the 'separated brethren' and treated them in his work as individuals just as fascinating and vulnerable as his fellow Catholics. He was not blind, however, to the evils of sectarianism and even in his comedies admitted its existence. (Notable exceptions were the scripts for the radio series, *The McCooeys*, written between 1949 and 1955, for particular reasons that will become clear later and, incidentally, demonstrating his command of the medium and his gifts in drama structure and dialogue).

In October 1932, in his twenty-second year, he was an observer of the 'Belfast Outdoor Relief Protests' that briefly blunted the edge of working-class sectarianism. The Belfast rates of 'outdoor relief' (minimal grants to those not yet in workhouses) were the lowest in the United Kingdom. Whereas Nottingham gave twenty-seven shillings per week to an unemployed man with one child plus a rent allowance, and Manchester twenty-one shillings, the Belfast Public Guardians allowed twelve shillings with no rent allowances. This relief stopped after a year, ludicrous when one considers unemployment, especially among Catholics, was endemic. One egregious member of the board complained of those seeking relief, '60 per cent are Roman Catholics from a particular quarter of the city' and the name of the chairman, Lily Coleman, has lived in infamy after her public remark about those who had large dependent families, that if they put the same effort into looking for work as they did under the blankets there would not be a problem.

A campaign organised by a communist breakaway group from the Northern Ireland Labour Party (NILP), led by Betty Sinclair and Tommy Geehan, was unusual in that its support crossed the sectarian divide, but characteristic in that it led to serious rioting with two deaths and that the Royal Ulster Constabulary (RUC) turned their attention to the demonstrators in the Falls rather than the equally vociferous campaigners in the Shankill. Relief was improved from eight to twenty shillings a week at the minimum level and from twenty-four to thirty-two at the maximum. Geehan described the result as 'a glorious victory' but the cross-community support was never again in evidence. Instead, in 1935, Belfast was the scene of further internecine violence with at least ten deaths and the deliberate eviction of Catholics from mixed areas. This was organised by members of an extreme splinter group of the Orange Order, known as the Ulster Protestant League, and if the response of government or local authority is any index, they had the tacit support of the authorities.

It was against this background that Tomelty, the young adult, grew to physical maturity. Riots, sectarian tension and mutual suspicion were endemic in the urban society, but they were intermittent. There was some work for a qualified painter, glazier and decorator, in Harland & Wolff and across the narrow seas in Clydebank and Barrow-in-Furness. Yet the decade was not known as the 'hungry Thirties' for nothing; the people who took to the streets in the 'Outdoor Relief' demonstrations did so in desperation. For many the choice was as stark as the workhouse or hunger. Whole families suffered from chronic malnutrition, the children especially from all kinds of deficiency diseases that should have been unknown in twentieth-century Ireland. The full extent of the physical and mental disabilities suffered by the poor of both persuasions would become clear when in the Luftwaffe raids of April and May 1941, the actual living conditions were made manifest. Bates may have dismissed them as 'unbilletable' but his (and that of his parliamentary and local government colleagues) was the responsibility for such inadequacy of welfare provision.

The effect on a young talented man was to root deeply and immovably in his psyche a loathing of bullying whether by officialdom, local and national, clerical, as in the many cases when arrogance and fastidiousness deprived the members of the cloth of the exemplary charity they should have shown, or familial, when economic necessity blighted even domestic peace. These, along with a special empathy for those afflicted with mental illness, formed the main planks of his literary structure and, combined with a rage at the vulnerability of the poor and dispossessed in dire need of state care, they permeated all his writings, comic or serious. His real enemy was poverty and he dreaded debt, regularly quoting Mr Micawber in *David Copperfield*: 'Annual income twenty pounds, annual expenditure nineteen pounds nineteen and six, result happiness. Annual income twenty pounds, annual expenditure twenty pounds ought and six, result misery.' With the coming of the social legislation of the Attlee government, some of the greatest deprivations were mitigated, especially in the spheres of health and education, and his later work acknowledges the improvements. The legislation also applied to Northern Ireland even though the Stormont government tried to lessen the Family Allowance payable because it clearly favoured 'those with large families' – handy shorthand for Catholics. (Westminster, as it turned out, would countenance no distinction between Northern Ireland and the rest of the United Kingdom.)

The perceived injustice against the nationalist minority also continued, but references in the books and plays, apart from *The End House*, are oblique and minimal. Tomelty had no remedy to offer but was content to make clear to the world the often rancid nature of political life in his native province. He was no preacher but an artist, implicitly echoing Hamlet's description of the role of the players: 'they are the abstract and brief chronicles of the time'. In spite, however, of the high seriousness of his approach to his work, he was not himself a depressive nor given overmuch to gloom. He enjoyed life, had a mischievous sense of fun, and deplored the mean, the selfish and the puritanical. This too, was part of his long *education sentimentale*. In spite of poverty, second-class citizenship and isolation, there was a remarkable amount of independent social life, some church-centred, some distinctly not.

Within easy reach of St Peter's were a number of cinemas that, though quite close to the city centre, did not charge city centre prices. As one walked up Divis Street towards the Falls Road proper, one could pass the Arcadian (1912) in Albert Street, the Diamond (1920), the Clonard (1913) and the Broadway (1936). A short stroll from the foot of Broadway was the rerun cinema, the Windsor (1935), and for the really adventurous there was the Majestic (1936) on the Lisburn Road across Tate's Bridge. Tomelty loved films and he was a regular visitor. One of his jokes was to ask the riddle: 'What's the difference between the Coliseum and the Grosvenor Hall?' [The first was a large city centre cinema and the other a place for religious services.] The answer given each time with the same glee was: 'In the Grosvenor Hall it's "Stand up for Jesus" and in the Coliseum it's "For Jesus' sake sit down."'

He also loved the Variety stage, going when he could to the 'gods' in the Opera House and the Empire. A friend, Gerry Jameson, remembers being taken by him as a boy to see Turner Layton (1894–1978), the bass singer and composer of such standards as 'Way Down Yonder in New Orleans'. He loved the circus and had staged one as a boy with his mates in Portaferry – with himself as ringmaster, naturally. When the circus came to town he would hang about offering to work in return for a free seat. Once, when the main attraction was a genuine 'Wild Red Indian', punters were warned: 'Do not feed with firewater – he go wild and scalp the town.' Tomelty and his friends regarded it as a sacred duty to ensure firewater was supplied. When they finally identified their quarry they asked him if he could use a pot of porter. The 'Wild Red Indian' asked them if there was a local bus so he could visit his married sister in Ballyhalbert.

Home-grown amusements included *feiseanna* held in the large parochial hall of St Mary's, dances, céilís in the Ard Scoil or St Paul's Hall, dances, socials, concerts and amateur plays. There were Gaelic games to play and teams to support and the even more popular soccer, with a first division club to support in Belfast Celtic (1891), with its home ground, ironically called 'Paradise', on the Donegall Road, ominously close to Windsor Park, the ground of Celtic's main adversary, Linfield. There were also libraries: the famously liberal Linen Hall and, much more convenient and absolutely free, the Falls Road Carnegie Library that was opened in 1902.

In a certain sense the confraternity devotions run by the Redemptorist fathers in Clonard monastery also constituted an entertainment. At the time, last Mass on Sundays in rural parishes provided, among other things, the best opportunity for randy young men to view, unmolested, the local talent. The confraternities provided the same opportunities to the youth of Belfast. It was not the main purpose of the devotions but the astute monks were fully aware of the lesser aspect. Hence the existence of a best-selling booklet written and published by the order called *May I Keep Company?* The answer from those young people who took the trouble to read it was a thundering 'No!' Tomelty was aware of the slightly odd nature of the institution in its socio-religious aspect and used it to strong effect in his novel *The Apprentice* (1953). Yet like the Gaelic Athletic Association (GAA) and the Gaelic League it had a strong cohesive role in forming the inner state that existed at a slight angle to the city as a whole. Apart from a weekly perpetual novena, the Redemptorists held twice-yearly retreats that concluded with soaring hymn-singing accompanied by brass and silver bands that were devotionally and emotionally memorable.

The foregoing paints, perhaps, too gloomy a picture of the Belfast of the '30s and early '40s. The sectarian tensions increased or died down with the change of seasons. Most people in the city just got on with living, antennae endlessly quivering but finding individuals from the other communities 'decent friendly fellows' so long as religion and politics were avoided as conversational topics, and there persisted an inevitable ignorance about the other community, because the common ground was so narrow. Tensions tended to increase with the marching season and the essential gerontocracy of the Stormont government found it useful, as had Lord Randolph Churchill (1849-95) in 1886, to 'play the Orange card'. In quantitative terms Belfast was no more 'violent' than Glasgow or Liverpool in sectarian matters. Most intelligent people regarded the whole need to 'stand up and be counted' as a bore or an intrusion into their personal lives. Yet Catholic and Protestant had atavistic programming that became part of their DNA. Tomelty could no more ignore his own conditioning than his opposite number on the other side of the Boyne Bridge but he found sublimation and an ultimate exorcism of sectarian demons in his work. His clear-eyed view of the province in his artistic heyday was expressed implicitly in all his writings and found its most precise statement in a sentence given to the tolerant, sophisticated water engineer, M'Greevy in the play *April in Assagh* (1953): 'I wish we had a plague of Religiosmyopia in Ulster for about ten years.'

Leaving school at twelve, Tomelty was apprenticed to his father to learn all aspects of the decorating trade. Not long afterwards, still quite young, he was awarded a scholarship to the Belfast College of Technology where a course of liberal studies (a fancy name for the 'three Rs for older pupils') was taken step by step with his vocational training. He first lived with a great-aunt, Rose Hamill, who came originally from Carrickmacross in County Monaghan, in Frere Street, one of the disappeared streets, then off the Cullingtree Road, that runs from the Grosvenor Road to Divis Street. He required some quasi-parental care but a great-aunt was hardly an appropriate companion for a talented growing lad. They parted company when, as a young man, he preferred attending a rehearsal rather than going to the Clonard confraternity, and his infamy was discovered. The prefect of his group, who appeared fictionally later in *The Apprentice*, wrote to tell his aunt of his non-attendance. When Tomelty came home from work the aunt and the letter were waiting for him. With a kind of instinctive dramatic touch, he carefully folded it into a spill, put the end of it in the fire and lit his cigarette with it. After that he lived in various digs 'All around the Loney-O', to quote a contemporary street song, including Dover Street that linked the Falls and Shankill Roads.

He acquired all the skills that a journeyman decorator was expected to have: mixing paints to reach the precise tint his customers desired; preparing surfaces with size and undercoats; working with acid on glass; and becoming adept at all aspects of the art of glazing and 'brush graining'. A contemporary fad was to have doors, especially street doors, painted to replicate freshly-hewn wood, complete with graining, age rings and knotholes. Experts could replicate the appearance of oak or walnut on ordinary deal. The pinewood was first covered with yellow ochre, to which a light, almost opaque, brown paint was applied. This stage was known in the trade as 'scumbling' and before it dried, steel combs of different tooth-widths and pieces of India rubber were used to score the surface into an acceptable version of the appearance of the superior timber, the yellow substratum showing through. *Real* craftsmen disdained any of these mechanical aids and did all the graining using brushes only. Tomelty learned this technique too and used it to good effect when the family moved into a large house at 217 Stockman's Lane that was sorely in need of expert decorative help. His brother Jim, who was the real genius of the family with paint, advised and supervised Tomelty's brush-graining of his study.

He worked as a painter in shipyards on the Clyde, in Barrow-in-Furness in Cumberland, and in the Island. It was while working in Harland & Wolff that he began to write. He recalled to Sam Hanna Bell (1909–90) in an interview for the *Ulster Tatler* that his workmates' reactions were practical rather than enthusiastic: 'Well, Joe, if it does nothing else it'll improve your handwriting!' In fact his handwriting was expansive and entirely legible. He did not ever seem to have considered setting up on his own, content to work for others at whatever contracts they had obtained. He painted the white traffic lines down the middle of College Street, practically in the city centre. And a persistent myth has him doing the same along Bedford Street, passing the Ulster Minor Hall that was to be the scene of future triumphs. At one period he was employed by a John Jameson who lived in Durham Street, that, running from Barrack Street to the Grosvenor Road, was essentially a frontier street at recurring times of what one of his characters in *Mugs and Money* (1953) called 'secretarian' violence. As was not uncommon, the assistant lived with the master. When Jameson died as a result of an accident near Whitehead, Tomelty had to find other work and new digs.

The experiences of these years of apprenticeship and articled tradesman he used to convincing effect in his second novel, *The Apprentice*. The description of the actual details of what such a position might mean has a raw authenticity and the asperity of the hapless Frankie's guardian/aunt may owe something to the experience of living with his great-aunt, Rose Hamill. Already he had developed the habit of jotting down overheard conversational phrases that struck him as wise, witty or even surreal. Once, his daughter Frances reported that she had heard one woman say to her companion: 'Y'know, dear, your legs are too far apart for you to wear jeans' and he wrote it down for future use. Some of his favourites were so sententious as to be practically meaningless. In the play *Mugs and Money*, Sarah Short, the Marleys' neighbour, announces that she would stop her daughter going to Hollywood, having won a beauty competition, if she were going 'to sup sorrow with the spoon of grief'. In the same play he achieves a comic effect by total mistranslation of Latin tags by characters anxious to impress with their learning and wisdom:

> BARNEY: I was always imbued with the maxim, 'Dulce et decorum est pro patria mori.' That's French, but freely translated it means,

'England expects this day that every man shall do his duty.'
STURGEON: That's 'Evil to him what evil thinks.'

Sarah's description of physical confusion as 'I'm running
sideways to get out of my own road', though complex, is, on mature
thought, perfectly logical. Did the ever-listening Tomelty hear
someone actually say it or was it his own?

Social life among the Catholic denizens of the Lower Falls was
inevitably and unselfconsciously parish-centred. In this it was
similar to other Catholic enclaves throughout the province. St
Peter's choir had, of course, a liturgical obligation to fulfil the many
weekly and seasonal ceremonies. Tomelty took lodgings with a
woman he had met in the drama society called Min Milligan, a
fateful move since there he found in her a leading actor for his
plays and in her daughter, Lena, his future wife. He had a fine
tenor voice that before the accident that fundamentally changed
his life had a greater range than that of his younger brother Peter,
who was a professional singer. Having ceased formal education at
the age of twelve, the ability to read music was not one of his
gifts. He had a remarkable ear to compensate for this lack, but
with increasing professionalism in the cathedral, he decided that
his lack of ability in any form of musical notation precluded his
membership. He was also noted as regularly wearing a red tie, in
those years a political rather than a fashion statement.

The finding of tolerable digs, even in those years of little
expectations, could be problematic, even for the less fastidious.
Tomelty retained dire memories of one landlady whose fingernails
were in permanent mourning. This distaste remained with him,
once leaving a restaurant because the waiter's fingers were
similarly adorned. Lena was briefly embarrassed but conceded
that he was perfectly right in his protest. Min Milligan was the
best of landladies. She was born in 1882, the year of the
'Invincibles' killing on 6 May of Lord Cavendish, the new liberal
Chief-Secretary, and the Under-Secretary, Thomas Burke, in
Phoenix Park in Dublin, as she frequently reminded her

grandchildren. Her father Ben Brierley, a soldier in the Cheshire Regiment, was posted to India but because the six-month-old baby had measles she was not allowed to travel with her parents but given to her maternal grandmother, Catherine Davey, to be reared. Granny Davey was a butcher, nothing unusual in those years when Hercules Street, the forerunner of Royal Avenue, was composed almost entirely of 'fleshers' as they were called then, and essentially a Catholic enclave.

It meant that her vocabulary, speech patterns and accent were that of the Belfast of the 1830s and even earlier. An umbrella was a 'gamp' as in Dickens's *Martin Chuzzlewit* (1844), dressing gowns were a luxury of the rich and nightdresses 'wrappers'. She 'tholed' pain when her head was 'stoonin' and when her Tomelty children went out to play they were told 'to mind the horses'. Bromide, that figures in both the *Barnum* plays, was an important part of her domestic medicine chest, as was Kali water. A sock filled with hot salt was an effective cure for a sore throat and bread and red soap poultices were used for drawing out 'matter' from infected wounds in those pre-antibiotic days. Her language was colourful but she would have blushed to think it might be thought obscene. Once, when Frances announced she would like to invite a boy to tea, Min said conversationally: 'Indeed and I knew his Granda – a carnaptious wee get and his Granny was an ignorant wee housel – a wee bit of a thing that you could have put under your arm and run away off down the street with.'

3

The Ulster Group Theatre

THE BELFAST OF THE MID-TWENTIETH century was no longer worthy, if indeed it ever was, of the title, the 'Athens of the North', given to it by the cultural radicals a hundred years earlier. Its success as an industrial city – Ireland's Birmingham or Manchester – and its preoccupation with product and profit precluded, many believed, cultural development. There were theatres, ranging from low music halls to the Grand Opera House, designed by the great theatrical architect Frank Matcham (1854–1920) and, as already noted, as the twentieth century progressed, many cinemas. There was little in the way of native material, both the Empire and the Opera House taking almost exclusively British circuit plays and shows. The first decade of the twentieth century had seen the establishment of the Irish Literary Theatre in the Abbey, Dublin, by W.B. Yeats (1865–1939) and Augusta, Lady Gregory (1852–1932), with the intention of, as their statement of intent put it, having 'performed in Dublin in the spring of every year certain Celtic and Irish plays, which will be written with a high ambition and so build up a Celtic and Irish school of dramatic literature'.

News of the venture stimulated the interest of such northern nationalists as Bulmer Hobson, Alice Milligan and David Parkhill who wanted to be part of the project. Cold-shouldered by Yeats but encouraged by Maud Gonne (1865–1953), they returned home determined to have an equivalent Belfast operation. Out of respect for the senior institution, they called their movement the Ulster Literary Theatre (ULT), adapting for local use the original name of the Dublin venture. They found playwrights in 'Rutherford Mayne' (Sam Waddell) (1878–1967), 'Lynn Doyle' (Leslie Montgomery) (1873–1961) and George Shiels (1886–1949), whose regular stream of plays would later help keep the Abbey solvent. The ULT's career lasted with intermissions for thirty years from 1904 until 1934 when, in Mayne's words, 'It died as it had lived – in penury.' It had contributed several plays to the canon, notably Mayne's *The Drone* and *The Turn of the Road* and one perennial squib, *Thompson in Tír na nÓg* by 'Gerald MacNamara' (Harry Morrow, 1866–1938). More significantly it stimulated a keen interest in and taste for local plays acted in local accents that persisted with amateur companies until the founding in 1940 of the next significant venture – the Ulster Group Theatre (UGT).

The UGT was formed by an amalgamation of three originally amateur companies and, like all *ménages à trois*, its day-to-day running could at times be awkward and even problematic. Its first tremulous signs of quickening were observed in 1937 when Tomelty was twenty-six and a member for some time of the am-dram group St Peter's, a company strongly associated with the pro-cathedral parish. His first successful attempt at drama, *The Beauty Competition*, would appear a year later. The ULT had never had a permanent home, using mainly the Grand Opera House in Belfast, the Gaiety Theatre in Dublin and, for its earliest offerings, the Ulster Minor Hall. The Ulster Hall had been built in 1860 with its magnificent organ installed in 1862. It was the city's main public hall and played its part in many colourful events, especially political. Its minor hall with independent access to Bedford Street was popular with the amateur companies that did not need a large auditorium and it was the venue for the presentation of some of the plays of the intervening years between the reigns of the ULT and the UGT, though the Empire and the Opera House were also used.

One of the amateur actors with ambitions to at least semi-professional standards of performance, if not of emolument, was J.A. Fitzsimons, a County Down teacher. As quoted by Sam Hanna Bell in *The Theatre in Ulster* (1972), he said: 'About 1937 after playing with amateur groups I realised we weren't getting very far – there was always a shortage of props and costumes and we could never accumulate enough money to dress our stages properly and we weren't learning an awful lot about play production.' The world of amateur theatre in any city is not very extensive and he soon was able to discover that many excellent non-professional actors and producers felt the same way as he did. Preliminary meetings were held in the house of Elizabeth Begley (1907–93), who had worked in a shoe shop and was a skilled actress. Among the interested parties who attended were James R. Mageean, John F. Tyrone (John Moss) and Tomelty. They decided to try to form a drama company known originally as the Ulster Repertory Company. Sixty per cent of any profits would be reinvested in the company and the remainder distributed among the players. Their first production was on St Stephen's Night 1938 in St Mary's Hall in Bank Place off Royal Avenue and they chose a popular favourite with a variable title, depending on location and current political climate. Its neutral title was *The Auction in Killybuck* but when it was originally written in 1915 it was called *The Pope in Killybuck*. The author, Louis J. Walsh (1880–1942), afterwards a district justice, was born in Maghera and the play's comic theme is the manipulation of sectarian attitudes for monetary gain.

Its success led to an increase in membership and a change of title to the Northern Irish Players (NIP) with R.H. McCandless as senior actor/director. Their manifesto indicated that they intended to produce plays of local and other Irish authors as well as the drama of the British and continental stage, and sought to foster and develop a permanent home for drama in Belfast. To flex their muscles, as it were, in June 1939 the NIP booked the Belfast Empire in Arthur Square and presented *The Letter* (1929) by Somerset Maugham (1874–1965), a steamy play set in Malaya involving adultery, murder and accusations of rape, and in stark contrast, the first production of Tomelty's first full-length play, *Barnum Was Right*. Then, no explanation of that title was necessary; Phineas T[aylor] Barnum (1810–91) was famous as the leading nineteenth-century American showbiz entrepreneur, inventor of the menagerie and the three-ring circus, the 'Greatest Show on Earth', and deviser of the neatest method of preventing overcrowding by directing clients to a sign marked 'Egress' where some expected to see another wild (female) animal. He is credited with originating the phrase: 'There's a sucker born every minute!' that gave Tomelty his title.

It was considered a trifle short and so they had, as a curtain-raiser, Anton Chekhov's (1860–1904) most famous short 'vaudeville', *The Bear* (1888). As ever, documentation about the UGT is virtually non-existent; it is tantalising that no copy of the Empire programme seems to have survived. One can see Tomelty in his element as the patient old servant Luka, delighted with the thaw in his widowed mistress, Elena Ivanovna Popova. The Empire venture made a loss that had to be borne by the members of the company by rule of constitution, but the existence of a new company and a new playwright had been established in the minds of the theatre-going public. *The Letter* had been directed by Harold Goldblatt (1899–1982), who, with a magnificent voice and a commanding stage presence, was one of the best-known actors in the city; and Tomelty's local fare by James R. Mageean. These first semi-professional productions manifestly lived up to their ideal of providing local and international plays for the citizens of Belfast, but they could not afford the self-indulgence of financial loss.

These aims turned out to be the same as those of another group called the Ulster Players, run by Gerald Morrow and Bill Hardie and his wife Nita, a couple who had successfully run the Curtain Theatre in Rochdale. Further, Mageean of the NIP had got to know Goldblatt and other members of the Jewish Institute Players and discovered a like ambition in them. There seemed to be no reason why all these interested parties should not form a company, however heterogeneous, and it was almost inevitable that Goldblatt, who had a keen grasp of finance, would become a senior figure in the enterprise. The greatest priority was the finding of a suitable venue and though the Ulster Minor Hall had disadvantages – the noises of public events in the main hall, which included hot gospelling, boxing matches and political conferences, could clearly be heard in the smaller auditorium – it was an appropriate size for the new company's projected audience.

The Belfast Corporation was not then known for having a strong cultural commitment, being concerned as ever to ease the burden on its bourgeois ratepayers. They had recent examples of losses in previous lettings to other drama groups and they were not at all helpful when Goldblatt began negotiations about rent. They insisted that they could not take a risk and set a possible rent of £6 a week. (That amount's buying power is the equivalent of £276 today.) The superintendent of the Estates Department still refused to grant the lease in spite of Goldblatt's offer of security. He did not finally yield until Goldblatt offered the £72 in advance, and secured a twelve-week booking.

And so the UGT came into being. At first it was an arrangement of convenience with each member of the troika granted the use of the theatre a week at a time. The very first production was of a comedy, *Storm in a Teacup* (1936), by the Scots dramatist Osborne Henry Mavor (1888–1951), who used the pseudonym James

Bridie. It was a satire on bureaucracy, a version set in Scotland of *Sturm im Wasserglas* (1930) by the German author Bruno Frank (1887–1946). It dealt with the complications that arose out of the refusal to pay a dog licence. The local papers approved, praising both Nita Hardie's direction and acting, and were glad to welcome a new theatre in which 'control and management are in the hands of men who have their roots in Ulster'. They went on to report that 'it will be their aim to develop native talent among players and authors too. It is a brave venture in times like these and one that deserves to be supported.' The hint of male chauvinism was embarrassing, in that, for the play reviewed, the 'control and management' were actually in the hands of a female. The 'times like these' referred to the fact that the 'phoney war' had become terrifyingly real. Within three months of the staging of *Storm in a Teacup*, France had fallen and 'Fortress Europe' was Nazi-controlled from the Arctic to the Mediterranean.

Apparently unperturbed, the press announced that 'next week Mr Goldblatt's company will be seen in *French Leave* and the week following the Northern Irish Players will make their bow with *Barnum Was Right*. A fine and happy prospect for all who value the living theatre.'

The full list of plays is instructive:

11 March: *Storm in a Teacup* by James Bridie and Bruno Frank
16 March: Mr Harold Goldblatt's Company in *French Leave* by Reginald Berkeley
27 March: *Barnum Was Right* – A Belfast Comedy by Joseph Tomelty
3 April: *Drama at Inish* by Lennox Robinson
8 April: Mr Harold Goldblatt's company in *The Chinese Bungalow* by Marion Osmond and James Corbett
15 April: The Northern Irish Players in *Mrs McConaghy's Money* – a play of Belfast life by Hugh Quinn
22 April: *Kind Lady* by Edward Chodorov
29 April: Mr Harold Goldblatt's company in *Love from a Stranger* by Frank Vosper

6 May: *The New Gossoon* – the well-known Ulster Comedy by
George Shiels
13 May: Ulster Theatre Company in *Many Waters* by Monckton
Hoffe
21 May: Mr Harold Goldblatt's company in *The Second Mrs
Tanqueray* by Sir Arthur Wing Pinero
28 May: Northern Ireland Players in *John Ferguson* by St John
Ervine.

There were clearly three separate entities taking turns every
third week. Goldblatt marked out his contributions by naming
his company for *French Leave*, a light comedy (1922), *The
Chinese Bungalow* (1940), a popular melodrama about the revenge
of a Chinese husband on his occidental wife for adultery, *Love
from a Stranger* (1936), a thriller about suburban madness based
on a short story by Agatha Christie by the actor Frank Vosper,
who played the lunatic lead, and *The Second Mrs Tanqueray*
(1893), the 'sensationally popular' drama about 'a woman with a
past'. The Ulster Theatre Company that had started the ball rolling
now presented *Drama at Inish* (1933), Lennox Robinson's glorious
comedy about the hilarious effect on an Irish seaside community
of a summer season of sombre drama featuring Tolstoy, Strindberg
and Ibsen, *Kind Lady* (1935), in which the eponymous kind lady
is menaced by a younger woman, and *Many Waters*, a sentimental
two-hander in which two elderly people reminisce about their
younger days.

These were the kind of offerings that any British repertory
theatre would be expected to provide. And in a sense they were
the sort of plays that George Shiels had found irrelevant and indeed
not greatly different from what was weekly available at the Grand
Opera House. In a letter, now kept in the Linen Hall Library's
theatre archive and quoted in *The Stage in Ulster from the
Eighteenth Century* (1997) by Ophelia Byrne, to McCandless on
13 May 1940 in response to the latter's request for a play for the
UGT, he expressed his reluctance to be associated with the venture:

> The pity of it is that I have always seen very vividly what an Ulster Theatre might be, and on various occasions my hope revived, only to be quenched again by some idiot, or set of idiots, talking in terms of *Charley's Aunt*. Instead of making Ulster drama the foundation of a Little Theatre, they make it a sort of stop-gap between third-rate English plays.

He did eventually acquiesce and in another letter written to McCandless on 6 February 1941, after a successful production of his play *The Jailbird* (1936), remarked that 'The Group had done very well.'

The Northern Irish Players' four productions essentially prepared the ground for what the UGT would become. Three of the authors became staples, Shiels, Ervine and the resident Tomelty. Hugh Quinn's realistic account of life in an ordinary Belfast working-class family, *Mrs McConaghy's Money* (1933), was well-known because of its popularity with amateur companies, and *The New Gossoon* (1930) was one of Shiels's best comedies dealing with the inevitable clash between old and young. *John Ferguson* (1915), a stark analysis of Presbyterian rectitude where a stern father is faced with having to deal with the rape of his daughter and his son's violent reprisal, was rooted in Ulster mores and appreciated as such but, though not necessarily appreciated nor ever lauded, it was certainly the presence of Tomelty in the company – a gifted playwright, who was also a fine actor and an energetic, painstaking general manager – that established the UGT on a sound foundation. He worked for the Group for ten years as manager but as he precisely insisted he was also booking clerk, ticket collector, cloakroom attendant, sweeper-up, scene painter, chucker-out, programme seller and actor – the last said almost as an afterthought. That list was not in any sense an exaggeration; Sam Hanna Bell once described to me an incident in the theatre when Tomelty in the box office was, let's say, roundly berated by a drunken American sailor and his lady companion because there were no seats left for a performance. He left the box office, picked up the offending client bodily, and deposited him outside in Bedford Street while his companion squeaked after them.

That adventurous springtime foray netted the UGT a profit of between £30 and £40 and gave the young company the courage to persevere, though the Hardies and Morrow withdrew their Ulster Theatre from the alliance.

Now, over seventy years later, their reasons for withdrawal are not clear. Perhaps the undoubted greater popularity and box office success of the four 'Ulster' plays suggested that the original commitment to the best of the drama of the British and continental stage might not be honoured. Certainly 'Mr Harold Goldblatt's Company', as labelled in the original press notices, ceased to exist as a separate entity. Of the plays staged in the Minor Hall from 1941 until the Group's sorry disintegration in 1960, six were by Tomelty, four by St John Ervine, three by George Shiels, seven by Patricia O'Connor, three by Jack Loudan, as well as Sam Hanna Bell's only stage play *That Woman at Rathard* (1955), based upon his novel *December Bride* (1951). Shiels had already written twenty-one plays and would live to write nine more. As 'George Morshiel' he had written *Away from the Moss* in 1918 and *Felix Reid and Bob* the following year for the ULT but he was essentially an Abbey dramatist, where his plays were sure to have comfortable runs. He did, however, admit later that the Group actors in his quintessentially Ulster plays caught nuances (and delivered them) that the Abbey actors seemed to miss, playing them for simple comedy. In a letter to McCandless on 28 November 1946 after the Group had done *Borderwine*, a play specially written for the company, he shows a slight impatience with the Abbey actors:

> There are always weak spots; the Abbey casts were always full of them, with bad interpretations to match. In the latter I should imagine the Group people are pretty sound ... drive home the point that plays that deal with contemporary life in this region are the only sure foundations on which to build an Ulster Theatre.

The same misapprehension marred the first production of Tomelty's serious drama, *The End House*. Even in the relative social and economic stability that came with the war, the Group Theatre management found it a play, not for the last time, too hot to handle and its premiere took place in the Abbey in August 1944. The Abbey actors were as skilled as their opposite numbers in Belfast, as their appearance in the film *Odd Man Out* in 1947 would make clear. Yet because of misdirection or a superficial resemblance in tone to Sean O'Casey's *Juno and the Paycock* (1924) or the unwarranted assumption that anything that Tomelty would write must be a comedy, *The End House* was played for laughs and accepted by the Abbey audience as a comedy, who then complained that there were not enough jokes.

The writer who welcomed the formation of the Group had praised it because of its daring 'in times like these'. By the autumn of 1940, Belfast had come within range of the Luftwaffe but for a while it was spared the visitation of terror from the air that afflicted London, Coventry, Glasgow and the cities and towns of the south coast. Surface air raid shelters that proved both noisome and unfit for purpose blossomed in practically every street. A great deal of adrenalin was generated and life seemed to take on a special edge. For the new season, the main Group attraction would be St John Ervine's Ulster comedy *Boyd's Shop* that opened on 16 September 1940. It was then five years old and had first been staged on Wednesday, 19 February 1936, at the Liverpool Playhouse with Michael Redgrave (1908–1985) as the Rev Ernest Dunwoody MA, a young Presbyterian minister 'on the make', and his future wife Rachel Kempson (1910–2003) as his fiancée Agnes Boyd.

It may be taken as a template for the essential Ulster play, with authentic witty dialogue, closely observed and rendered Ulster characters and speech, the presumptuous and arrogant put-down, the wildness of youth tamed, the wisdom of age triumphing and true love winning in the end. Compared with the latent savagery of *Barnum Was Right* it was reassuring, even cosy, and intensely popular. The publicity suggested that it was 'a simple comedy in which the essential kindliness of the Ulster people appears'. Goldblatt said of it: 'It really started us, gave us an insight as to what our policy should be. The major portion of our work should be the Ulster play.' As Shiels was to the Abbey, Ervine and Tomelty were to the Group, but no play took the city's fancy like the story of rival grocers and rival suitors in the typical Ulster village of the fictitious Donaghreagh. The name was constructed from two common elements in Irish placenames: donagh (*domhnach* = 'church') and reagh (*riabhach* = 'grey'), an acceptable Irish Everytown until Brian Friel's invention of 'Ballybeg'. It was revived seven times during the Group's twenty-year existence and was set for a record run of more than fifteen weeks when it was halted by the catastrophic air raid of Easter Tuesday, 1941, when up to a thousand people died and more than half that number were seriously injured.

That evening of 15 April 1941, the Group played to a full house and the four-act play was almost over when the alert sounded. Tomelty had landed the plum part of the unctuous Dunwoody and in a contemporary cast photograph he stares coldly at the camera. His steel-grey hair was inappropriate for the part and so he dyed it black. This led to trouble when the Group went on tour to Liverpool since the hair on the photograph on his travel identity card photo did not look right. Men did not admit to dyeing their hair in those days. As manager of the theatre, he would have seen to the shepherding of the audience out of the theatre as they went fearfully home. He, then aged just thirty, made his way back to his digs in 95 Dover Street and watched the city centre disintegrate into fiery chaos. He wrote a vivid description of the bombing for the *Irish Times*, discussed elsewhere. The play was one of the most popular ever staged in the city. By the time of its fourth revival in 1944, it was estimated that at least 42,000 people had seen it and there were several outlets about the city called 'Boyd's Shop'.

The 1941 run continued successfully after the threat of air raids had ceased. Incredibly a remarkable number of theatregoers turned up on the Wednesday evening after the raid even though the theatre, undamaged, was closed for lack of actors who could not make their way to Bedford Street because of the piles of rubble, burst water mains and exposed electrical cables. So popular had the play become that for many people it became their first pleasurable theatrical experience. One very pious old lady who had never been to the theatre before had been persuaded to attend. She enjoyed the play thoroughly but as she made her tearful way home, she announced that the raid was God's punishment on her for having to do with the Devil's playhouse.

The Ulster Group Theatre had arrived and succeeded in its ideal purpose of finding an Ulster voice not only in the locutions of its actors but also in the dialogue provided for them. It 'discovered' new actors and new dramatists, presenting, over its score of active years, fifty original plays. The actors and the dramatists were already there but the UGT's very existence stimulated them and gave a focus to their talents. In the sphere of acting, as well as McCandless, Goldblatt and Tomelty himself, the talents of such people as Min Milligan, James Young, Elizabeth Begley, Doreen Hepburn, J.G. Devlin, Denys Hawthorne, Maurice O'Callaghan, Harry Towb, Allan McClelland, Patrick McAlinney, James Ellis, Margaret D'Arcy, Colin Blakely, Bee Duffell and Stephen Boyd gave it great distinction and when the fabric crumbled, most found acting careers elsewhere. Lena Tomelty once said that even if you didn't like a Group play, the acting was always wonderful. Yet though the actors excelled in ensemble playing, it was not a happy company. Jealousy and envy were rife and deliberate upstaging was not unknown.

Considering his worth to the company as manager, actor and playwright, it must be said that the management treated Tomelty badly. McCandless continually disparaged the *Barnum* plays, dismissing them as: 'Scratch your arse for a laugh!' He was kept on tenterhooks for their decision about whether to stage offered plays – this treatment for a writer of profitable long-running plays, providing a lot of the finance that kept the enterprise afloat! Members of the public would berate him jokingly, as he sat in the box office, that his stuff was too popular, ran too long and deprived them of theatrical variety. Appearing in an Ulster play, not necessarily his own, he had the capacity to change lines on stage and win more laughs. McCandless loathed this practice and used to listen for unexpected laughs when Tomelty was on. One night, sitting backstage, he heard extra laughs while Tomelty was on. It was a box set and the only way to see what was happening on stage was through the fireplace. He knelt down and put his hand on something soft, caused by a recent visitation of the theatre cat. The actors onstage were amused to hear a disembodied voice gasping from the fireplace: 'Ach, cat shit!'

When Tomelty was chosen, in 1951, to take part in Tyrone Guthrie's season of Festival of Britain plays, instead of hearty congratulations for him and the reflected glory on the UGT, the founders resorted to threats of exclusion. In fact, having found a new film career, he never acted for the UGT again, though they were glad to continue to stage his plays. It allowed him, however reluctantly, to develop his dramaturgy and did 'discover' other dramatists, especially Patricia O'Connor whose plays *Highly Efficient* (1942) and *Select Vestry* (1945) lifted a critical lid on primary education and the Church of Ireland. When the first was seen to be highly critical of the system of Ministry of Education rewards – the title of the play was also the name of a desirable classification, often obtained by less than the best pedagogical practices – the sell-out houses were full of cheering teachers and scowling HMIs. One of these latter, a known bully, tried to storm his way into a full auditorium past the official on duty – Tomelty. Seeming to believe that he had power outside the classrooms he terrorised, the inspector demanded a seat, as by right. He was informed, as Tomelty recalled the incident, that there were no vacancies and should even the King of England (then George VI) and the Pope of Rome (Pius XII) come up the stairs hand in hand (a wonderful, surreal picture), they too would be turned away. Two young teachers, observing the confrontation from the bar, insisted on buying the talented and courageous front-of-house manager a drink: 'Mr Tomelty, that man is the bane of our lives!'

Other dramatists who had premieres at the Group were Hebe Elsna, Janet McNeill and Stewart Love. An ominous special case was *The Bonefire* (1958) by Gerard McLarnon (1915–97), whose play about the hopeless love of a Catholic sailor and his Protestant sweetheart whose attempted immolation on an Orange bonfire on the night of the 'Twelfth' proved too 'controversial' for Bedford Street and was transferred triumphantly to the Grand Opera House, bringing with it its stars, Elizabeth Begley, Colin Blakely and James Ellis. It was a second foray into Ulster theatre by Tyrone Guthrie as director. One playwright who almost qualified as a UGT dramatist was Sam Thompson (1916–65). He was born in Belfast and apprenticed as a painter in the Island in 1930. Encouraged by Sam Hanna Bell, he had written such radio features as *Brush in Hand* (1956), *Tommy Baxter, Shop Steward* (1957) and *The General Foreman* (1958). That year he met James Ellis in the Elbow Room, a pub in the Dublin Road much favoured by BBC staff and Group actors. Ellis had been appointed that year to the board as assistant artistic director to Goldblatt, who found the entitled intrusion of members of the Council for the Encouragement of Music and the Arts (CEMA) because of its financial subsidy, wearisome.

Thompson, whose language offstage as well as in text was trenchant, to say the least, told Ellis: 'I've written a play but you won't touch it.' Ellis read *Over the Bridge*, a strong account of sectarianism in the shipyards that Thompson had experienced as a youth in Harland & Wolff and immediately approved, as did most of the members of the reading committee. The board, strongly influenced by the chief CEMA representative, J. Ritchie McKee, a member of the ruling Unionist establishment, rejected it because it would cause 'trouble'; there was no sectarianism in the shipyard. Their statement was a classic piece of Unionist think:

> We are determined not to mount any play which would offend or affront the religious or political beliefs or sensitivities of the man in the street of any denomination or class in the community and which would give rise to sectarianism or political controversy of an extremist nature.

It was essentially the end of the UGT since no cultural entity could survive under the threat of such censorship. It was reminiscent of the bleak days of a decade earlier when the hands of Sam Hanna Bell and John Boyd (regarded by the BBC Northern Ireland establishment as essentially subversive) were tied as to the nature of the talks and features they hoped to broadcast and when there seemed to be total unanimity between Ormeau Avenue and Glengall Street. However, 'the times', as Mr Zimmerman would later note, they were 'a'-changing'. Ellis and Maurice O'Callaghan resigned from the board, disappointed at the *trahison des clercs* of McCandless – Goldblatt had already resigned. Ellis immediately formed a company called Bridge Productions and produced and directed – and acted in – the play in the Empire, where, in a theatre that dwarfed the Minor Hall, it ran for six triumphant weeks. Ellis had no difficulty in casting the play since many of his Group colleagues auditioned for parts, risking their own careers. They included J.G. Devlin, Harry Towb, Catherine Bingham, John McBride, Thompson himself as Archie Kerr, a trade unionist, Ellis as the leader of the mob – and Tomelty as Davy Mitchell, the staunch trade unionist who is murdered at his bench by the mob.

A critic wrote about this performance 'Tomelty's character,

doughty, fair-minded Protestant trade unionist Davy Mitchell, was exquisitely observed ... ' *Over the Bridge* was a success for Thompson and Ellis but the Group was finished, another brave venture that had come to grief, wrecked on the reefs of official Belfast Philistinism.

4

Campbell's Coffee House

THE RELINQUISHING BY TOMELTY OF HIS brush, except for scene-painting, and the involvement in work that occupied him at night, left the days free for writing and broadcasting. On nights when he was not onstage he could write in a large freehand (as his heavy typewriter was at home in digs) stories, novels and further plays. John Boyd had been appointed Talks Producer for BBC Northern Ireland in 1946 and used his often problematic post to advance many literary careers. He persuaded Tomelty to write stories for the medium.

They got to know each other around the voluble tables of Campbell's Coffee House in Donegall Square West. Friendship between the pair soon grew with Tomelty dubbing the serious-minded Boyd as 'Pastor', both behind his back and to his face. Campbell's was the sober Belfast equivalent of what would have been a poets' pub in a more sophisticated milieu. Its informal membership included writers as well as Tomelty: Denis Ireland (1894–1974), Sam Hanna Bell, 'Richard Rowley', the pseudonym of Richard Valentine Williams (1877–1947), who published Bell's first book, the collection of stories, *Summer Loanen* (1943), and Jack Loudan, the Armagh playwright who was to be Amanda McKittrick Ros's biographer; artists such as Willie Conor (1881–1968), Padraic Woods (1893–1991), Gerard Dillon (1916–71) and George Campbell (1917–79).

Bell afterwards described the coterie as 'young men consumed with a terrible thirst for knowledge'. They were all left-wing in politics, Bell selling *Socialist Appeal* and *Labour Appeal* at street corners, Boyd a member of the Communist Party. One of Sam's colleagues in the Air Raid Precaution service (ARP) also helped sell the political literature. This was Brian Moore (1921–1999) who would make a splash in the literary world with his first novel *The Lonely Passion of Judith Hearne* (1955) and whose 1965 novel *The Emperor of Ice Cream* paints an unforgettable picture of the Easter Week Blitz of 1941. Tomelty, now in his early thirties, shared the politics and the general delight when the venal Belfast Corporation was dissolved for malpractice in June 1942 and replaced by a three-man Commission that ruled the city until late in 1946. He went so far as to include a reference to it in his contemporary play *Right Again, Barnum* (1943). He was always slightly suspicious of politicians, and the permanent rootedness of the Unionist party at Stormont and the Corporation before and after the Commission he found tedious and frustrating. He had already written five plays including *The End House* (1944) partly in protest at Dawson Bates's Special Powers Act, referring to the Special Branch as 'Bates's Harriers'. Though even greater literary achievement was imminent, his world-vision – how he would have chortled at the word *Weltanschauung* – was already established and it would continue to be adumbrated in these future plays and novels.

First he had a pathological hatred of bullying, of pupils by teachers, of employees by bosses, of patients by doctors, of the public by officialdom, whether by civil servants or their armed forces, the RUC and the even more execrated B-Specials, of

charges by nuns and, most wounding of all, of flocks by their
religious pastors. These were not, of course, blanket
condemnations of whole classes of society, but there was clear
evidence that such oppression was widespread. The most
vulnerable were, of course, the poor, who in spite of resilience,
optimism and industry were never likely under the existing social
structures to do more than subsist. With the coming of the Welfare
State in the late '40s their condition improved a little and due
recognition was given to Aneurin Bevan (1897–1960), the father
of the National Health Service, the advantages of which were also
applicable to Northern Ireland. In *Mugs and Money* (1953), the
juvenile lead, Gugs Marley, doing a face massage, is warned by
her mother Martha:

> For Moses' sake, child, mind your top set doesn't drop out. That's
> the third set you've had since Nye Bevan started giving them
> away. You'll have to pay for the next.

It was a deliberately comic and topical line but it is an implicitly
damning one of the social conditions that families like the Marleys
had to suffer. Tomelty's hatred was based on his own experiences.
As an adult he was fearless but when he gave his hero Frankie
Price in his novel *The Apprentice* (1953) a debilitating stammer,
especially with the tricky initial letter 'f', he remembered
schoolboy humiliation by a teacher. He had been forced to declaim
Mark Antony's speech over the dead body of Caesar and could
not get past the first letter. The obscene repetition caused a lot of
un-innocent merriment in the classroom. He made Johnny Fowls,
the main character in his story 'Confession', suffer the same
humiliation.

Perhaps the most pathetic and yet strangely interesting, to him,
of the psychologically downtrodden, were the mentally afflicted.
They continued to fascinate him, not in a morbid or even
pathological way, but as troubled creatures, placed at an angle
oblique to what the world takes as normal. It is Tomelty's portrayal

of that dread possibility of madness that shows best the effectiveness and control of his writing as witnessed by such elemental characters as Kathrine Quinn in *All Souls' Night*, Miss Price in *The Apprentice* and Winnie in *Red is the Port Light*. In his work there is the slow unveiling of corrosive madness. For example, in *Red is the Port Light*, he builds the tension to the climax, where the final sight of Winnie, her mouth stained with grass and dandelions, swinging an open razor is profoundly shocking and disturbing.

The empathy with the lonely, the deprived and the weak marched hand in hand with a burgeoning sense of humour and of confidence in his own mental stability. By the time he was established as general manager at the Ulster Group Theatre at a wage of £2 a week, he was a fully paid-up member of the Campbell's 'salon'. He would have been aware of the intention of Sam Hanna Bell and his ARP boss and flatmate, Bob Davison, to publish a 'little magazine', the Belfast equivalent of *The Bell* produced by the maverick Peadar O'Donnell (1893–1986) and edited by Sean O Faolain (1900–91), Ireland's leading man of letters. Since its inception in October 1940 it had caused a stir, not only in literary circles in the otherwise somnolent neutral Free State, but also in political, social and even clerical ones. The list of contributors reads like a *Who's Who* of contemporary Irish writers and included two stories by Bell, three by Lynn Doyle, three by Michael McLaverty and a piece on Belfast slang by Tomelty in July 1941.

He would have taken part in the preliminary discussions – the coffee house rang perpetually with talk and an indulgent management made no attempt to evict the talkers. He was almost certainly used by Bell in his determination to make 'Pastor' Boyd become its editor, as the man best equipped with a critical faculty and more leisure than the rest. All would have known the relevant admonitory quatrain by Keith Preston (1884–1927):

> Of all the literary scenes
> Saddest this sight to me:
> The graves of little magazines
> Who died to make verse free.

There would have been no great optimism. The Belfast emulators could not compete with a much sought-after Dublin monthly but were happy to try to get at least one number out. Bell, in a piece written for the *Honest Ulsterman* No 74 (September 1979/January 1980) as part of a symposium on 'The War Years in Ulster', wrote:

> While stoutly disclaiming that a 'literary renaissance' was coming up over Ben Madigan, we thought that writers would be glad to see their work in print. The pervading isolation must have engendered some feeling of comradeship among us. I can think of no other plausible reason, for at that age we should have been concerned with our own work and not [with] editing the work of others. *Lagan* was the success it deserved to be and appeared annually till 1946.

The title was chosen by Bell, a nod towards the river in the basin of which the majority of Ulster people lived and which had the essential advantage of being non-denominational. (*The Harp*, an earlier suggestion, was wisely dumped.) Bell also provided the anthological indication in the subtitle, 'A Collection of Ulster Writing', and remained the main driving force for the four annual numbers that appeared. Many of his colleagues contributed to the first number, including W.R. Rodgers, Maurice James Craig, Robert Greacen, John Hewitt, Michael McLaverty and Roy McFadden. Bell contributed a story, 'The Broken Tree', while the editor published one of his own stories, 'Dying Day', exploding and half cobbling together again the myth of family happiness. Tomelty's contribution, in a not uncharacteristic stygian mood, was concerned with the lonely and the gullible. He called it 'Destiny', though its theme was not directly about fate or karma, but after the famous waltz composed in 1912 by Sydney Baines

(1879–1938), another measure of the way that music saturated his life and work.

A young RUC constable called Smoll is pleased when his application for transfer from the village in which he is stationed to Belfast is approved. The village is one with:

> ... the bulk of its people Catholics, the remaining handful ... Protestants. The majority, he knew, hated him ... the Protestants humiliated him.

At first he is pleased with the city patrols in the company of Krey and Stooker, senior members of the force, since the personnel of 'Fruithill' Barracks prefer to 'parade in threes and fours'. The name given to the police station is deliberately mischievous. The nocturnal wartime patrols checking that no light showed through the obligatory blackout window blinds and ever on the lookout for members of the IRA suggest that the manor was a working-class precinct in West Belfast. The actual Fruithill, then almost in the country, was too bourgeois to merit such attention from the law. Smoll remains a misfit, lonely and romantic, teased by his older colleagues and ill at ease on patrol where the renascent IRA is more dreaded than Luftwaffe bombs. He fantasises about a pretty girl he meets regularly on his beat, associating her with the waltz of the story's title. Nerving himself to make his feelings clear he uses a duty call to her digs to speak to her, only to discover that she is on the game.

> She was lovely and he loved her. Now he could go back to the country. It did not matter about Protestant or Catholic. She was a woman he loved. He could go anywhere with her. He found now the answer. All he wanted was this woman. No one could humiliate him or embarrass him if he had her. And he was confident. Her smile made him so.

When he discovers from her landlady that 'she is making a randyboose of my wee home' and finds her in bed with a soldier, 'her red blouse stained with black', his collapse is almost physical:

> He was thinking about her red blouse, with its black stains, just like poppies that were dying. They too had black stains. They were withering and soon their dark eyes would be peppery dust. Another shout of 'Whoopee' came from the house. Then he heard her laughing, laughing wildly.

It is a typical Tomelty story, full of compassion for the lonely and the inadequate but unable to offer a solution.

'Confession', the story contributed to the second number of *Lagan*, is an early take on the misery associated with stammering and the debilitation and degradation it can inflict. Printed nine years before he gave the theme a fuller treatment in *The Apprentice* (1953), it is much darker and more relentless than the novel. Its opening paragraph is stark indeed:

> My name is Johnny Fowls and my age is twenty-one. If you met me in my rags sitting on a bank waiting for the cows, you would think I was twice twenty-one, for my hair is grey, my feet are bad and my shoulders are gathered, and if you asked me the time of day, I'd answer you with a grunt.

In its precise description of Fowls's condition the piece is more case history than story, though the writer is more emotionally involved than a clinician would dare to be. (The reader cannot help but notice Tomelty's regular habit of giving his characters odd names). Though perfectly sound mentally and physically otherwise, his near total inability to communicate renders him effectively less than human, a jeer in the eyes of his fellow students, teacher, stepfather, mother and finally a shopowner, Fry, well-known for his shabby practical jokes on 'tramps and tinkers, and made them look silly … ' In despair and driven literally out of his mind by repeated mockery, Fowls stabs him in the stomach with a garden hand-fork.

It is something of a relief when Fowls is sent to Borstal for five years. There he makes a friend and is treated in a not unkindly way by the Brothers. His agony remains and though outwardly docile, he wrestles each night with his Catholic conscience because he feels no remorse for his attack on Fry. When his time in the institution is up he finds a job as a menial on a dairy farm, with his bed in the byre. Always a loner and finding temporary peace in roaming alone about the mountains, he makes the acquaintance of a shepherd whose potent mixture of reassurance and poteen helps him find a personal gait of going and even the prospect of romance with perhaps:

> ... a servant lass over in Andrews' with notions of men in her head, and there's another beyond in Megan's, and if it's a fair-haired one you want there's a lassie kicking her heels up in Wilsons'.

Yet even this quasi-solution is darkened by Tomelty almost perversely, as the last sentence makes clear:

> I miss him, for a few days after that the police came and took him away for making poteen.

The stories with their serious, unflinching approach to Ulster life were just the kind of thing that John Boyd had in mind for *Lagan*. There is little comfort in them but they have a strength that was not popular in the generally escapist reading matter of the time. Not that Tomelty's preoccupations were permanently with gloom and failure. It was around then that the popular *Barnum* comedies were conceived and though the Marleys never quite succeed they are equally not totally conquered by the hard life in the slums. By now his preternaturally sensitive and retentive ear had garnered enough phonic information to render Belfast demotic speech appropriately for the stage.

It is interesting that his 'note on Belfast slang' appeared in *The Bell* in July 1941, less than a year after it started in October 1940. In the opening number Sean O Faoláin in an editorial entitled 'This is Your Magazine', asked for contributions from everybody and anybody: 'You know a turn of the road, an old gateway somewhere, a well-field, a street-corner, a wood, a handful of quiet life, a triangle of sea and rock, something that means Ireland to you.' Tomelty answered O Faoláin's call in a characteristic way by finding parallels between Cockney rhyming slang and the usage he had picked up in Belfast: 'Rory O'More' for door, 'Craigavad' for bad. The true Bow Bells denizen on the dole might use 'How d'ye do?' for 'Buroo' (bureau) but for his counterpart in Belfast, there was only one 'Buroo' – 'for he says he is on the Brian'.

There are many more examples in the light-hearted piece and it leads one to wonder what he would have made of the information that the rhyming slang for the dish 'curry' is 'Ruby' from Belfast's own Ruby Murray. Language is part heritage but it is also evolutionary. In an *Ulster Tatler* profile by Sam Hanna Bell, Tomelty told a story illustrative of his delight in linguistic adaptation. At one part of his career as a painter he used to meet a girl who had got a job as a maid in one of the grander houses on the Malone Road, an area proverbial for refinement of the native Belfast accent. She greeted him with the observation that 'it's very coul', and he agreed. He did not see her for a couple of weeks during which time the weather had not improved. When next they met he spoke first, saying, as he claimed, 'It's still very coul,' and she replied, 'Yes, it's beastly cold.' As he said to Bell: 'And that's what a fortnight up the Malone Road can do to you!' *Si non è vero, è molto ben trovato* for it pinpoints his own preoccupation with how people express themselves.

Tomelty appeared again in *The Bell* exactly a year later contributing a paragraph to a symposium called *The Best Books on Ulster* for which a number of northern writers were asked to make recommendations. Tomelty's list is comprehensive and pertinent. *The Wayward Man* by St John Ervine, a novel that is 'a portrait of the average working Protestant in Belfast'; *Mrs McConaghy's Money*, a play by Hugh Quinn, 'a glimpse of the Belfast that was and the Belfast that is'; 'The descriptions of the Mourne district in *Private Road* [a novel by Forrest Reid] are perfect; it also deals with what we call the Upper Ten.' He recommended *Lost Fields* by Michael McLaverty for its glimpses of 'the famous Falls Road, its Catholic people, their habits, their awful fatalism'. He also advises readers to consult a pamphlet by Denis Ireland, *An Ulster Protestant Looks at his Own Land.* Finally, with an irresistible awareness of Irish politics, he asks, 'if we are not confined to the Six Counties I would like to place a novel by Peadar O'Donnell on my list'.

Of three other newspaper articles also written in the mid-1940s, two for the *Belfast Telegraph* consider aspects of theatre in Ulster and the third, done for the *Irish Times*, gives a graphic first-hand account of the Easter Tuesday Luftwaffe Blitz. The first has the slightly irrelevant title 'There is No Such Thing as a Stage Ulsterman', probably imposed by a sub-editor, and is redolent of the fact that the war news was at its gloomiest. In it he considers recent criticisms of the stage's limitations in conveying the industrial might of Belfast and its 'war effort'. However he reminds us that:

> The playwright is not interested in them as workers in a shipyard but as human beings. The shipyard man who boasts of the number of rivets he can sink in an hour is good enough for a talk on the wireless but on the stage the audience would find him a positive bore – unless he is in love with the landlady – which is just the point the playwright would take up.

The second has the title *Plays*, and subtitle, 'Over 200 are written in Ireland yearly', and in it he considers why so few of them make it to the stage. It is a fine piece of diagnostic writing by a professional totally at ease while talking about his craft. Most aspiring playwrights 'haven't the foggiest idea of what constitutes a play. Their idea of a play seems to be a string of lifeless sentences'. He lists various types of aspirants: the one who just wrote it 'for the fun of writing', the one who would improve a Chekhov curtain-raiser by bringing in a melodeon player; the snob who 'tired of the infernal Ulster kitchen' writes on the cover that, all the people in his play are 'educated and speak good English'. The trouble is, says Tomelty, 'while their English is good, they have nothing to say'. He has to dismiss a play that uses a whole act to discuss the result of a golf foursome: 'Even Noel Coward could make little out of mashies and niblicks.' A plot summary in which an Englishman escapes from a house in Shanghai after killing six Chinese, all of whom were armed with knives, would upset Hollywood 'and they have more brass neck than we have in Bedford Street'. Unstated but implicit in the whole funny piece is that good dramatists, like other good artists, are not plentiful. He concludes: 'Any country can breed civil servants and shorthand-typists but geniuses do not arrive so frequently.' It was a gentle put-down but there was no doubt that the thirty-one-year-old who wrote it was at last confident of his own standing.

5

Lady, Be Good

O N THE WHOLE, THE BRIGHT YOUNG intellectuals of Belfast did not have a bad war, the three nights of terror and tragic loss excepted. The Luftwaffe did not return after the night of the great fire in May 1941, with the concentration of incendiary bombs doing much more fabric damage than during Easter Week but taking fewer lives. There was still the threat of another visitation and so fire-watching in the Ulster Hall continued. In the *Honest Ulsterman* number mentioned earlier, one of the contributors, the poet Roy McFadden, left a series of short takes in prose that capture the heightened atmosphere of the time:

> In Ballymacash John Boyd shrewdly slanted pedantic eyes across manuscripts for *Lagan*, while the evening porridge plumped and fretted on the range.
> Sam Hanna Bell, embattled in his tin hat, proffered good advice on the use of the stirrup pump.
> – Joe has been reading Chekhov, Sam Hanna Bell said, rubbing the war wound of his helmet weal.

> – Tell your friends, Joe Tomelty wheedled from the stage of
> the Group Theatre at curtain call …

Though there was rationing and eyes scanning the heavens at
the sound of aeroplane engines, there was still fun to be had –
crack – spelled correctly in those untendentious days. These
youngish Turks were self-consciously different, favouring a kind
of uniform of sports coats often in Donegal tweed with leather
elbow patches, hopsack shirts, tweed ties and green corduroy
trousers. Clothing was rationed as well as most other things and
without the correct amount of coupons one could not buy a suit.
However 100 miles to the south and 150 to the west, the Free
State beckoned with plenty of butter, eggs, meat and drink – and
tweeds. Boyd, Bell and Tomelty once went on a jaunt to Dublin
and at some stage on their train journey, Tomelty's fly-buttons
came irrevocably undone. (Zip-flies were virtually unobtainable
then). He sat in his window seat, a book covering the gap, while
his two mates scoured the train for a woman with a young baby
who could give them a large nappy pin. It was an anecdote retold
many times and a reference to it may be found in the canon of
Irish literature. Bell, in his book *Erin's Orange Lily* (1956) – an
imposed title, which he loathed – has an uproarious riff about the
casual way that new tunes were given titles by their composers.
In memory of that gaping fly he invented one himself. In a rare
moment of gaiety in the generally sombre *December Bride*, when
describing the Ravara Fête he has the local piper set up for dancing
at the crossroads:

> The piper stepped into the middle of the road and fingered a
> jig, *Tomelty's Verdant Breeks.*

Of the three close friends, Boyd, the youngest, was the first to
give up bachelorhood when he married Elizabeth in 1939. Bell
did not wed Mildred Reside until 1946, by which time Tomelty
had been married for four years and was the father of a daughter.
His wife was Lena Milligan, the daughter of his fellow-actor and

landlady, Min Milligan, known to her grandchildren as 'Granny Minnie'. 'Lena' had been christened Catherine, though the family called her Cathleen except that her brother Jack, older by six years, couldn't say the word and was able to manage only the final syllable; she was Lena from that out. It gave legal trouble later; she once had to sign an affidavit to state that Catherine and Lena were the same person. Elsie Ivory, a lifelong friend, confided in Lena that she had met Tomelty in town in a café one day and that he was singing to himself the Gershwin song 'Lady, Be Good', that had been featured in a 1941 film of the same name. The next day Lena told her that she was engaged. The news was greeted with surprise in Portaferry because Tomelty's family 'never thought the "Big Fellow" would ever marry'. Fr Watson, the parish priest, who had known the Milligans when he was a curate in St Peter's, was able to reassure them that he was lucky to get Lena.

The ceremony took place on 3 August 1942 in St Peter's. It should have been a typical austerity wartime wedding; the bridegroom's trousers did not have had turn-ups, as was the usual design until clothing rationing came in. The bride wore a silver-grey dress while the bridesmaids, Ellie Johnston, Lena's closest friend, and Elsie Ivory, had dresses of dusky pink (the fabric smuggled from Dublin). All the dresses were made by Elsie's sister Kitty who was a skilled dressmaker. Tomelty's brother Jim was best man. No one owned a camera even if film had been available but the *Belfast Telegraph*, aware that the author of *Barnum Was Right* (1939) and the general manager of the Group Theatre was being married, sent a staff photographer. (Tomelty's salary of £3 a week was increased that day by ten shillings.) Unfortunately the photographer went by mistake to St Peter's on the Antrim Road so no pictorial record of the event exists. It was a serious mistake since the Antrim Road St Peter's was clearly Church of Ireland. (The bride maintained a characteristic cheerfulness over this disappointment as she patiently waited some further years before they could afford an engagement ring. When the time came, the ring had the traditional five diamonds). The breakfast was held in the Union Hotel near the city centre and it was there that the bridegroom spent the night before the ceremony. The owners, a pair of sisters called Johnston, were great supporters of the Group.

They spent their honeymoon in Wynn's Hotel in Abbey Street in Dublin, travelling by the Great Northern Railway to Amiens Street, taking with them their ration books, as many of their fellow citizens had done to escape briefly from wartime Belfast. It was not quite the Ritz, especially during the Emergency (as the neutral Free State called the war) and maintained for years an atmosphere of austerity. Still, Dublin with its bright lights, theatres, cinemas, ice-cream unavailable at home, and in the Gaelic phrase *togha gach bi' as rogha gach dí* ('with all manner of food and drink') except, of course, tea (rationed to half an ounce per adult per week) they managed to survive. They returned to Dover Street but soon were able to move to a house by themselves. Lena's brother, Jack Milligan, and his wife Annie had left their home in 81 Iris Drive, a street that runs parallel to the lower Springfield Road, and were living in Crossgar, a village six miles from Downpatrick. The newly-weds were delighted to move in and they became noted in the street for their eclectic repertoire of songs featuring Lena's fine contralto and Tomelty's rich tenor: standards like 'Smoke Gets in Your Eyes', 'These Foolish Things' and Irving Berlin's plaintive, 'What'll I Do?', operetta and traditional Irish songs. One of them, 'The Singing Bird', was to provide the title and theme of one of Tomelty's finest plays.

They were keen too on Broadway musicals; when Rodgers and Hammerstein's *South Pacific* opened in London in November 1951, they saw the show and added 'Some Enchanted Evening' to their informal repertoire. They saw *Porgy and Bess* in Paris while Tomelty was filming in 1954. When it was felt that the risk of air raids was past, Jack and Annie returned to Iris Drive and so the Tomeltys moved back to Dover Street. It was when they lived there that their two daughters, Roma and Frances, were born in

1945 and 1947 – the actual deliveries took place in the Antrim House nursing home on the Cliftonville Road at the corner of Clifton Park Avenue. Frances became very ill with pneumonia in 1948, a potentially fatal disease in those years of the early NHS and primitive antibiotics. The family doctor, the much-loved Catherine McNeill, advised that conditions in Dover Street were unhealthy. They bought at auction a bungalow in Stockman's Lane, then virtually in the country. To the children it seemed to be quite a walk from the trolleybus terminus at Fruithill Park but when they were sent to primary school the link with the Lower Falls was maintained. They attended Dunlewey Street, not far from Clonard Monastery, run by the French Sisters of Charity, who were known as 'Butterfly Nuns' because of their extravagant Breton headdresses. It was a shortish walk, less than half a mile from there to Granny Minnie's house in Dover Street where they went for lunch. Appropriately enough they called the bungalow St Catherine's and it was their home until 1957 when, after Joe's accident, a move to 217 Stockman's Lane, a much larger house, in fact a Victorian villa, on the other side of the road, was considered by their medical advisors to be more suitable for the convalescent.

The bungalow years were the period of growing achievement and fame. Especially after the success of *The Passing Day* in 1951 and the beginning of his film career, Tomelty was as often away as at home but he was able to bring the most exotic gifts to his daughters, then six and four years of age. Tomelty preferred to travel by steamer rather than by air and it was always an occasion of excitement and delight as they saw him off at the Belfast docks because they were allowed Coca Cola in the elegant original bottles, not long imported from America, in the departure lounge. Over the next four years they were given Easter eggs from Fortnum and Mason's with their names embossed in chocolate and giant lollipops a foot and a half long. The wicked little ladies would tell their friends that they had bought them for sixpence in

Murray's, a shop at the top of the Lane on the Andersonstown Road and the poor proprietor and his assistant were driven to distraction. Sweets had only just 'come off the ration' and anything was possible! One little friend of Frances said enviously: 'I bet yous have paper petticoats', then the last word in desirability. Apart from these occasional treats the children were not indulged; their wise mother and wiser grandmother would soon knock any fancy notions out of their heads. After their father's accident frugality was necessary but even before that it was instinctive. Both parents – especially the father – had experienced poverty in their young lives and had no intention of spoiling their children.

Roma and Frances gradually realised that there was some purpose in their father's inexpert typing, done with one finger of the right hand while a cigarette was held in the left. He wore a special jacket of a coarse green material with fawn cuffs and just before the children's bedtime, each was allowed to sit in turn on his knee while they typed their names. Often, probably as a necessary break from writing, he would bounce them on his knee to nursery rhymes and then walk with the child's feet balanced on his instep. He was as they remembered him 'always a kind and gentle daddy'. His kindliness was not confined to his family; he had a long list of clients who to Lena's despair called regularly at the Stockman's Lane bungalow for 'a little help'. Frances remembered an occasion when they were having a day out at the zoo at Hazelwood; a group of children from St Patrick's Orphanage, known locally as 'home boys', were there too. Tomelty bought his charges ice-creams and sent them to play while unobtrusively he paid for twenty-one ices for the visitors and spent the time pushing them on the swings. He was also responsible for boys from the orphanage getting parts as extras in *Odd Man Out*.

In time he felt he could afford a little car – and bought a tiny Ford from the breadman, BLV 520. It tended to become pretty cramped when the four Tomeltys, Granny Minnie, Cousin Ellie and the dog got on board. No wonder they claimed that at times they had to lose some of the passengers when they reached a steep hill. There was always a dog. The first was called Barney and he had followed Tomelty home from the Group one night, and successive places were taken by strays or gifts of members of unwanted neighbourhood litters. One of the longest-lasting had been Mickey, a tough, grey, curly-coated beast who gave the impression of being pure-bred; his mother had been Min's bitch Tessie and one of Tomelty's regular comments was that a Kerry Blue had caught up with his mother. In old age, a nightly walk with the current dog was an essential part of Tomelty's regimen. He always referred to the current dog as 'the oul' fella' and addressed it more in admonition than in respect as 'Sir', as in: 'Get down, Sir!' when it struggled for ownership of Tomelty's chair.

The family went each summer to Carnlough, a resort halfway up the Antrim coast on the beautiful Carnlough Bay. Then with a population of scarcely more than 1,000, it was half the size of Portaferry and essentially the place chosen by Tomelty for the family's summer home. In an interview with Richard Dimbleby, then the leading BBC television personality, he said: 'I'm a County Down man but I take my holidays in County Antrim.' He was anxious that his city-born and -bred daughters should have 'roots' outside the urban sprawl. George Shiels lived there and David Kennedy, his mentor and the man whose opinion he most respected, spent the summer there and suggested he find a house in the area. Carnlough became the family home for the months of July and August for sixteen years, and the Antrim glens (with Glencloy running right down into the bay) and the North Channel counteracted the ill-effects of being pent-up too long in the city. The first year was spent in the house of Hessie McNeill (the ultimate Glens name!) at the harbour but it was felt that because the children were still small and there was no garden, the danger of falling off the pier could not be ignored. After that they rented a house from Tommy and Brigid Campbell, situated on the

'Ballymena line' (the road from the village to the Glens capital fifteen miles away).

It was a small semi-detached cottage, with four rooms and a scullery. The kitchen was very much the dayroom, in constant use, with a large range, scrubbed wooden table and sensible kitchen chairs. The parlour was tiny and crammed with cumbersome Victorian furniture: a large round table with a walnut veneer, discoloured and partially 'raised' and blistered by damp, unsafe for placing crockery upon. There was a red plush chaise longue, two large fireside chairs and four upright dining-chairs in the same plush material but wounded by protruding springs. The adults rarely entered it but it became a handy playground for the girls on wet days, not unknown in that part of the world. Like all summer places the cottage had elastic sides, accommodating the parents, Roma and Frances, Granny Minnie, cousins Kathleen, Patsy and Jackie Milligan, and in the summer of the accident, 'the Ma' and Eileen. The parents had one of the two bedrooms while the rest slept where they could.

BLV 520 was an important part of the summer holiday plans; they used it for excursions to Cushendun, Torr Head, Ballintoy, Ballycastle and sometimes as far as the Giant's Causeway, dismissed as 'too touristy'. They could not, however, resist a visit to the Carrick-a-rede rope-bridge on the north Antrim coast that connects the mainland near Portballintrae to the rocky island where salmon is usually plentiful in season. They were fascinated and a little scared as they watched local fishermen shoot a shark.

Before BLV 520 was purchased with such formality, they arranged for a Carnlough hackney driver to collect them and the equipment for the stay. A significant item was a large theatrical skip into which they packed bedclothes, holiday gear, including buckets and spades, water wings, delft and cutlery, after they had ousted the dog who always jumped in for fear he might be left behind. The distance from Belfast was forty miles and the route was by Larne and then up the spectacular Antrim Coast Road.

Now it would take less than an hour but in the late 1940s before motorways were considered it was quite an expedition. Indeed by the time the expedition reached the hamlet of Ballynure, thirteen miles away, there were cries that the car should be stopped 'for the dog's sake'. The company usually included Granny Min, who, famous for her hats, made a point of wearing her very best for the journey.

There was no lack of intellectual company and there were lots of local events in which Tomelty happily took part. It was to Carnlough he came directly from the set of *Hobson's Choice* (1954), startling his friends by his appearance. He was not allowed to shave his facial hair for reasons of continuity and the white hair, ginger beard and black whiskers amused the townsfolk but 'affronted' his pre-teen daughters. He fished, usually in the sea with the local doctor though at times they tried with permission the Glenarm River in Lord Antrim's estate. Tomelty loved fish, especially bought at the harbours along the coast as the boats came in. The women of the house accepted the wild salmon he brought home but refused to handle lobster, which he had to cook himself. After his accident, the effect of his brain injuries made his balance uncertain and he boated less. Inevitably, when the children got a bit older he acquired a dinghy that was unsuitable for the open sea and was kept in the harbour.

Like his brother Peter, who regularly made the journey to Portavogie, the important herring centre on the outer coast of the Ards Peninsula, to meet the fleet as they landed, he was fascinated by the unsaleable exotic species that lay at the bottom of the boats and were usually thrown back into the sea. Tomelty once bought a conger eel that was chopped into manageable chunks by the fishermen. He had not the horror of most landsmen of mackerel but insisted that the backbone be removed and the flesh eaten immediately. He loved game, especially hare, and did all the necessary surgery, including the preliminary bloodletting.

Journeys in BLV 520 were shortened by the ever-increasing

Tomelty family song repertoire. There were songs specifically used for car journeys, which in their endless repetition were more appreciated by the children and the adults, such as 'Lloyd George Knew My Father', 'A Mother Was Chasing Her Boy Round the Room', 'Michael Finnegan', 'When George II Was King, My Boys' and a song that originated with Tomelty's agent Freddie Joachim, himself a Jew, that began 'The First Jew Went to Heaven?' and could have 100 repetitions.

For their 'parlour' and fireside repertoire they learned 'McCafferty', the ballad about the Irish soldier who shot two officers who had made his life miserable, chanted 'The Croppy Boy', the 1798 ballad, the first verse of which gave Tomelty the title of his most popular play, *Is the Priest at Home?* (1954), and tried to sing their great-grandfather's party piece, 'When I Was a Lad', Sir Joseph Porter's patter song from *HMS Pinafore*. When the girls were old enough not to be shocked, he propounded his theory that the popular parlour piece 'The Next Market Day', collected and arranged by Herbert Hughes (1882–1937), was not as decorous as our parents might have thought. He believed that the 'three guineas' obtained by the 'maid going to Comber' were earned not by selling 'three hanks of fine yarn' but rather more vigorously. He did not, as far as is known, set about applying the same textual analysis to another song of deliberately erotic intent, 'Kitty of Coleraine'. One of Tomelty's intended projects was the writing of a ballad opera as John Gay (1685–1732) had done so successfully with *The Beggar's Opera* (1728). Because of his accident it was one of many unrealised ambitions but I can think of no one better equipped by nature and training than he for the purpose.

They continued to rent the summer place even after the accident though the house was not in any way suitable because of the catastrophic change that was visited upon the father – at least in the summer of 1955. (This was their seventh visit to their summer place and they continued to come to the same house for a further eight years until the girls grew too old). Tomelty had barely come out of his coma when off went the family as usual to Carnlough. It was a gallant – and probably therapeutic – move. One of his unoriginal but often uttered apophthegms, that first impressed then embarrassed and finally charmed the children, was: 'Logic is a poor swimmer in the sea of emotion.' It certainly was in this case but Lena's decision, and it was on her that the main burdens fell, came from an instinctive realisation that some kind of re-establishment of normality and coherence was necessary to 'save a life' – the cry from the early play, *The Elopement* (1939).

Joe's parents, James - known far and wide as Rollickin' and Mary Tomelty.

Min Milligan (L) 1902 The Shaugran, (other actress unknown).

Mary Tomelty in later life with Tomelty's brother Jim dressed for a concert. He was a fine baritone.

A young Lena with friend Elsie on the beach at Sheeplands.

Lena.

Carnlough July 1950.

With the dreaded beard which all the family hated.

With Frances.

A younger Frances at Granny in Carnlough.

The Tomeltys in 1951.

At the first formal of daughter, Roma, Peter and Min (1968).

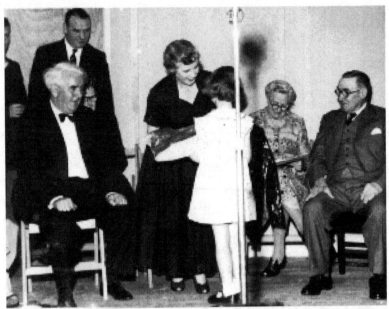

Tomelty adjudicating at opening of the Medway in Portaferry.

Y.P. Ball Plaza with late brother Eugene and Susan Colton, (March 1950).

Re George Shiels—

Shiels was tied to a wheelchair. That denied him the
freedom, one needs in any theatre, if one wants to write.
I recall him telling me. "How lucky you are to be
working in a theatre." When we ─────── ─────
─── I ────── ────── He told me, he didn't
think there was so much in the part" I'm
afraid, I was my usual naughty self and did a
─── of ad libbing─ But it ─── me that
had he been able to visit theatres his work might
not have been so ────────. He would have
learned the ─── and don'ts

I'm sorry love, but my typewriter has died.
no ─── for it. excepting I have written, it
did me well

Regards to Colin
lots of love
Paddy

at one time we were not allowed to say "─── in the Belfast
BBC. I had to say — "my folly" and I ──── ─── ────
for a day ─── a ───

Tomelty's 1976 letter to Roma.

The Painter.

With co-workers.

Lena and Lily Ritchie (The Ma) with cats! and Mickey, Joe's dog..

Min aged 70 when she was playing Aunt Sarah in The McCooeys.

Lahore 1955.

Roma, Frances, Lena, Jimmy Ellis, Rachel, Joe, Colin and Ruth at 80th Birthday launch of Bust by Carolyn Mulholland.

With John Knipe (AUDF) and committee members of Bangor Drama Circle, Mayor of Bangor and Roma who adjudicated the Bangor Drama Festival.

Honorary Degree, QUB. J.J. Campbell, Joe, Lena, Colum (later Father) Campbell.
Harry S. Gibson.

Last public appearance with Lena at rehearsal of The End House.

With Richard Dimbleby at Belfast Castle.

With the painter Willie Conor. Decorated by Dr Jim Ryan.

6

The Long Genesis
of *Mugs and Money*

AS WE HAVE SEEN, TOMELTY'S FIRST venture into drama was a one-act play called *The Beauty Competition* written in 1938 for St Peter's Drama Society, of which he was a member. The script, with instructions appropriate to radio drama, was afterwards submitted successfully to BBC Northern Ireland and repeated a month after the initial broadcast. A farcical comedy with a predictable plot, it already showed signs of the author's mastery of the speech of working-class Belfast. A notebook in the Tomelty archive in the Linen Hall Library contains probably a final corrected longhand draft of the original, labelled 'A Farce Comedy in One Act' by Joseph H. Tomelty. (The initial 'H' used here to give an extra gravitas to the dramatist's title stood for Hogan, a family name). The characters' names are given in red and the whole has the appearance of a fair copy to be preserved for posterity, which it thankfully was. (The same notebook holds a tantalisingly unfinished piece of writing, partially in dramatic dialogue, called *The Witch*. It is tantalising in that no further development of the idea has been discovered; it has characters with slightly offbeat names like Thaney Tod and Lucinda Lane – a typical Tomelty touch. A character named Lucinda would reappear in a later play, *April in Assagh*). A comparison with a companion item from the archive, a radio script of *Barnum Was Right*, with pencilled emendations, including deletions and additions, shows a gradual evolution and improved dramaturgy.

The main plot is the same in each of the three redactions. The scene is the kitchen of a small terrace house in working-class Belfast. The father is an old soldier in all the senses of that phrase, idle and work-avoiding, and recovering from a night's drinking at an Old Comrades reunion. His wife Biddy does her best to keep the family, a son Willie John and a daughter May, afloat. The son plays little part in this early version and May exhausts herself trying to keep the peace between her sharp-tongued mother and feckless father. It is she who enters for the beauty competition (entry fee ten shillings) for which the prize is a Hollywood contract. She has scrimped and saved to collect that substantial sum of money and leaves it safe under the mantelpiece clock.

By the time it had become ready for broadcasting there had been slight changes to the characters' names. The feckless father, first seen, or rather heard, as suffering from a hangover after a regimental dinner for veterans, has become Rabby Marley and it is clear that the reunion was of Great War veterans, that had finished only twenty years prior to the time of writing. Equally 'under the weather' is his mate Barney Brudge, a painter and decorator with cultural pretensions, speaking intimately of Sir Joshua Reynolds and John Ruskin while having the reputation for hanging wallpaper upside down. He blames his condition on the fact that 'I was leaving a fellow to the boat last night … ' An unfortunate bipolarity that is liable to turn him into a street corner preacher, especially outside his favourite pub, has not yet surfaced. He acts like a less vocal Belfast Joxer, even to the point of claiming that his scheme for obtaining a 'cure' is a 'darlin' idea'. Indeed one can find echoes of O'Casey's *Juno and the Paycock* (1924) in Rabby and Biddy as less rounded versions of Captain Boyle and Juno. O'Casey influences are even more obvious, as we will discover, in *The End House* (1944) with Ulster equivalents for Johnny and Mary Boyle in Seamus and Monica, owing much to the O'Casey originals.

The comic sub-plot concerns the 'borrowing' of May's ten-shilling note by the pair of rascals, thereby depriving May of her chance to win the prize. In *Barnum Was Right* she becomes Gugs – Willie John could not pronounce 'Gertie' and so Gugs she remained. They use Hughie, a refuse collector, to buy drink but he allows the bottle to slip and break. (Then the euphemistic term for the messenger's occupation was presumed appropriate; later a more confident Tomelty would have used the term 'brock boy', who collected organic refuse to feed one of the many small piggeries that were widespread at the time). The 'darlin' idea' had Rabby simulate faintness while the drink had to be obtained as the remedy – hence the emergency use of Gugs's entry fee. Another undesirable crony, a 'returned Yank' called Dark Davey, enters with enough drink to act as 'hairs of the dog' for the revellers and asks in return that they fry prime pork sausages he has brought with him. He too is hustled out at the distant approach of Biddy and she is positioned holding the frying-pan just as the *deus ex sausage-machina*, the rep for the company, arrives to reward her for 'using the product'.

The money allows Biddy to recompense May and have a little for herself. With typical resourcefulness she sends a forgiven Rabby with the pan to a friend's house so that she too may claim the cash. May is inconsolable that she will not be Pansy Petal (her chosen name for films) nor the 'Mary Pickford of Ireland' as Barney grandiloquently dubs her. There is a nice piece of period detail in that the other Hollywood stars mentioned, Greta Garbo and Janet Gaynor, were once 'silent' but had made it into the 'Talkies' era. It is after the final revelation that the beauty competition was an elaborate confidence trick that Rabby is given his line about Phineas T. Barnum from which the second title was generated, though the word attributed to the American was 'sucker': 'There is a mug born every minute.'

Encouraged by Larry Morrow (another member of a massively talented family), Tomelty extended *The Beauty Competition* as a radio play for BBC Northern Ireland in 1938 and called it *Barnum Was Right*. Rabby's character as a lazy, fantasising loafer is emphasised and the weary nagging of his wife, now called Martha, greatly elaborated. As he moans with neat topicality: 'Hitler and Mussolini are not the only dictators.' Her view is that Rabby's idea of a fully-furnished house is one with a corkscrew in every room. Dark Davey from the original play has been jettisoned in favour of Sergeant-Major Scotty Sturgeon, a drinking pal of Rabby. They chant the same mantra as Rabby and Dark Davey did in *The Beauty Competition*:

> In pubs we've often met and therein drunk our fill;
> In jail we've never met and hope we never will.

And Rabby is only too pleased to associate himself with Sturgeon's announcement: 'The major said he would take it as an insult to the past glory of the regiment if ivery man was not happily drunk. I can tell you nobody insulted him.' Gugs's entry fee is now a pound and the stranger reveals himself as Sam Sausage from the renowed firm of Poloney and Poloney. As noted earlier, a stage version of the radio play was the first offering of the Northern Players, staged in the Empire theatre. It was repeated the following March in the new home of the newly-formed Group Theatre at the Ulster Hall. No copy of the text has survived but its strength and popularity urged Tomelty to update it as *Mugs and Money* in 1953. Ten years earlier, not long after the terrible Belfast Blitz, he visited the Marley family again with *Right Again, Barnum* (1943), underlining the largely unmentioned facts that Rabby is Catholic and an ex-member of the Ancient Order of

Hibernians (AOH), while Martha is revealed as a member of the Women's Orange Order.

The author was now one of the best known Ulster writers and actors, with two novels, at least seven plays and many radio scripts to his credit. The play is still a comedy and he uses some of the same kind of jokes that had worked in the earlier versions. He was now forty-two and supremely confident in his literary ability. The same theme of Gugs's betrayal and that of many other postulants by a confidence trickster is dusted off and made newer. The competition is for Miss Ulster and the preparations for the event are detailed. Willie John, now unutterably camp, tries to indicate to Martha why his really quite plain sister might have a chance in the competition:

> WILLIE JOHN: No, ma, it's beauty of character they're looking for, beauty of line, and bone structure, etcetera …
> MARTHA: Son, dear, that's Greek to me.
> WILLIE JOHN: That's just exactly what it is, ma, Greek … you know like classical.

Later on he has to admit that her ankles are too beefy – 'like a Mullingar heifer' – though she has given them a course of 'pummy-stone' (pumice). When he fixes a guinea contract for her in which her hands are to be photographed for an advertising campaign, it turns out that her hands, fingernails suitably mutilated, are to be used for the 'before' pictures.

There are many local references and a few in-jokes: 'He has more faces than the Albert Clock.' Willie John wants nice stories for the magazine he works for: 'Not ugly stuff, you know, like that fella Hanna Bell and the other fellow Tomelty writes.' A much more abrasive Martha continues to upbraid her ever more feckless husband and Willie John's nerves cannot stand the bickering. She calls the painter Barney Brudge 'Barney Google' from the 1922 jazz song by Rose and Conrad that has the words 'Barney Google with the goog-goog-googly eyes'. When accused by Rabby that if he died she'd 'have an oul' buck in my place in six months' time', she replies, 'I had one poultice all my life and I wouldn't have another for all the gold in the Bank of England,' to which he topically replies: 'Not that there's a hell of a lot of gold there.' Another contemporary reference is to Nye Bevan and his National Health Service in the heady days when teeth and spectacles were distributed free and freely. A reference to Oedipus (according to Barney a 'Roman Emperor or something') is explained by Willie John as 'classical … all very Queen's University-cum-Malachy's Old Boys, if you know what I mean'. Barney's pretensions to culture are further revealed (as in the earlier version) when he claims that he was 'always imbued with the maxim, "Dulce et decorum est pro patria mori." That's French, but freely translated it means "England expects this day that every man shall do his duty."' Sturgeon insists that it means: 'Evil to him what evil thinks.'

Gugs's chosen name for her Hollywood career is now Dolores del Monte; Sam Sausage is now the rep for 'Messrs Skin & Poloney Limited, the world-famous makers of superb sausages' and Martha's windfall award is now 'the rich sum of one guinea'. She, of course, insists that 'there's not a Saturday night in life that we don't have it. My husband here raves about it.' And she is anxious to inform him that it was her sister Maggie McKittrick, who lives at number twenty-three, 'put me on to them'. Rabby is sent up the entry still without his trousers (it is, after all, true farce) to Maggie's to anticipate Sam Sausage's visit. She is able, having got her guinea, to dispatch him further to her friend Jenny, who also scores. When Sam announces that he is off then to Greencastle, they consider sending them to friends there as well but they decide they can't manage it. It is farce but local and kindly intended and cracks like: 'Don't be like an Ulster cabinet minister – don't be a rubber stamp!' would have pleased some of the capacity audience, as would: 'She looked the Markets type from about Eliza Street.' Mangled sentences like

'Where folly is bliss it's ignorance to be wise' were what the theatregoers expected.

   Mugs and Money was developed as a farce and all the usual ingredients are there: *déshabillé*, near misses, running and hiding, last minute reprieves and final collapse. Yet the characters, however caricatured, are not caricatures but real people *in extremis*. In spite of the nascent Welfare State they are poor and underprivileged and luxury plays no part in their fretful lives. Their creator is careful to underline their resourcefulness, energy, and, in spite of many complaints, their ultimate lack of self-pity. Even though it is a comedy he cannot ignore the social and political background to their misadventures. Willie John's idea for a series of articles in his magazine about his Hibernian father and Orange mother has to be aborted. He suggests they enter for what he calls the Finaghy Filch, his misheard Belfast version of the Dunmow Flitch. This prize of a side of bacon was awarded each leap year since the twelfth century to any couple who, kneeling on hard stones in the churchyard of Little Dunmow in Essex, could swear that there had been no marital rows in the interval nor wish by either party that they were single again. Yet in spite of his nervy ebullience he has to admit that: 'The crusader ... here in Ulster has an awful time ... the crusade to bring Orange and Green together.' The Finaghy Filch has to be abandoned because 'one of the boys put out a placard announcing it and, here dear, they broke his windows'. The police cannot find the culprit: 'You see, he lives in a mixed locality' – a neat encapsulation of the Ulster situation.

   Tomelty's courage in facing the sectarian nature of his adopted city was equalled only by his chutzpah in his treating of homosexuality. Willie John was the first overt homosexual on the Irish stage and the treatment of the character was mature and sophisticated. Making him unmistakably homosexual, he avoided extremes of camp behaviour and, in James Young, he had the actor who had the experience and skill to carry it off. Tomelty was always amused at the euphemisms used to cover what was then an illegal way of life. While gay actors in Britain were said to be 'very musical', in Belfast the term most in use was 'very good till his mother'. He treasured conversations overheard on the tram and trolleybus and used them appropriately in his work and was very pleased when Elsie Ivory, his wife's lifelong friend, recalled a conversation she heard on the Falls Road trolleybus. Two men were discussing a posh new barber's shop in Chichester Street called Rottger's. One said: 'I was there last week. You want to see it. The guy shaved me – hot towels, brilliantine, aftershave lotion. I was waiting for him to give me a kiss and ask me to go to the Plaza.' (For many years the Plaza was the Mecca of all the city's dancehalls).

Mugs and Money was Tomelty's last urban play, appropriately morphing out of his first. Poverty, described in *The Apprentice* as a cancer, was under at least palliative care, and sectarian tensions at their most muted. He had done well by the city but there was no further need to celebrate it on stage. He had already become established as the city's working-class laureate thanks to his brilliant, long-running radio soap *The McCooeys*. He had been writing 8,000-word weekly scripts since 1949, a task that only ceased because of the accident. By 1953 he felt that he had done enough of the kind of naturalistic, light comedy that he did so well and which seemed to the outsider effortless. Other aspects of his art had begun to interest him more and formed the basis of his aesthetic future when he could spare the time from a busy film career and the weekly chore of recording the doings of his atypical, idealised Belfast working-class family.

7

Early Plays

FTER THE SUCCESSES OF *THE BEAUTY Competition* and *Barnum Was Right*, Tomelty began tentatively to enlarge his dramatic vision. He had shown an obvious talent in the writing of comedy but realised that other modes and themes presented an interesting new challenge. By 1939, when he was twenty-eight, he had written *The Elopement*, a shortish play for radio tailored to suit programme schedules and broadcast in February of that year. The cry: 'Save a life!' told first to him by a sea-going uncle remained with him as a kind of hopeless wail of despair and in this grim play it is repeated three times in the penultimate speech. He was to use the triple wail again in his greatest play, *All Souls' Night* (1948), as the ghost of Stephen Quinn reveals the hopeless cry he made for rescue. Compared to the multi-layered structure of that later masterpiece, *The Elopement* is straightforward with a simple storyline of the death of two young lovers by drowning as they try to escape from a forced marriage and a manslaughter charge.

In spite of its story being fairly straightforward, there are many indications of early forms of later preoccupations. Molly's Aunt Rebecca is a kind of first run of Kathrine Quinn in *All Souls' Night*, frugal to the point of miserliness, admittedly cruel to the dying sister, Martha, who was Molly's mother and obsessively anxious to 'sell' the young woman off to a rich farmer, Adam Kilty. Martha 'married for love':

> REBECCA: She went against my own father and mother and married your father – a penniless clown of a tradesman from the mainland … When the typhoid of the '90s came to the island, she was weak, so weak with hunger that she had no strength in her body to fight it. That was love for you!
> MOLLY: You could have brought her food.
> REBECCA: Yes, we could, but she went against her own father and mother. Doesn't the Good Book say that it's a sin to go against your parents?

The listeners must already have realised that beauty could hold no plea against this rage, in the face of such bleak rectitude. Rebecca, Kathrine, Frankie's aunt in *The Apprentice* (1953), Sebina Sirk in *Idolatry at Innishargie* (1942) and others are strong women, the married ones with weak or henpecked husbands, recur regularly in Tomelty's plays. Even his comedies have versions of them, Martha Marley in the *Barnum* plays being an example. They contain elements of his own mother and of his great-aunt Rose Hamill who was his first uncompromising landlady in Belfast. Not that these sorely-tried ladies were the monsters of his creation but certain aspects of their characters he incorporated in them in an attempt to understand their asperity. His mother Mary, often at her wits' end having to deal with seven children, with a husband known as Rollickin' James, whose popularity and skill with his fiddle may not have made him an ideal breadwinner, had forbidden books in the house as time-wasting and Rose and Tomelty clashed over priorities: the Clonard perpetual retreat versus a play rehearsal. With his powerful imagination he could visualise how these decent people could morph into monsters given certain mental or financial straits.

Another recurring element was an interest in lunacy, sometimes gentle, virtually harmless, sometimes murderous. These pathologies played their parts in future novels and plays. In *The Elopement* the wounded party is Matthew Mann, the relentless Rebecca's husband who had been sectioned by his wife and had spent two years in an asylum. He is weak and fearful of a second incarceration (' ... my words are just like dying leaves ... They fall but no heed is taken of them ... I never had much say – it's worse now. Since I was away that time she treats me as if I was a wee boy. Yes, but without the affection.') and does what he can to help Molly to escape the unwanted match. It was he who introduced her to the heady pleasures of poetry. Rebecca, of course, totally disapproves and in an excess of what the Scots call *unco guidness*, wants him to cut down the hawthorn hedge that has been a traditional lovers' trysting place for years. He refuses, instinctively beginning to quote a line from *The Deserted Village* by Oliver Goldsmith, the single book that was allowed to stay in Tomelty's keeping:

> The Hawthorn bush, with seats beneath the shade
> For talking age and whisp'ring lovers made.

He is, of course, prevented from continuing by his wife with 'You're at that oul' poetry again.' J.B. Keane (1928–2002), the Kerry playwright, is on record as stating that *All Souls' Night* gave him the stimulus to write his first play, *Sive* (1959); that has poetic elements to it but it is interesting that, like *The Elopement*, it too has the theme of death as preferable to a forced misalliance.

Idolatry at Innishargie was first staged in the Minor Hall on 20 April 1942, a year after the Luftwaffe Blitz that had left the Ulster Hall virtually undamaged. The part of the eccentric Dendy Dale, who takes tales from Greek mythology as literally true and continues to find Proteus, the sea-god, in every seal that surfaces, was played by the doyen of the Group, R.H. McCandless, Tomelty was Sam Sirk, the smallholder who also accepts these wonders as gospel and Liza Lowry, the free-spirited drunken neighbour, by Min Milligan. The part with its combination of simplicity of character and stubborn will suited Tomelty well. The location is maritime with the flotsam and jetsam of the sea combed by the people for profit, and the news, regularly reported, that vessels have run aground on shoals is regarded as a legitimate opportunity for 'prog':

> Didn't Wallace Mackin make a son a doctor and another a clergyman on the money he pilfered from the Dutch sailors that were drowned in Knockinelder Bay?

The play, which has elements of comedy, even farce, is hard to categorise. The Sirk family with son Johnny and daughter Hessie are essentially simple people with lives not much above subsistence. Much of their land is waterlogged and their small stock of animals in need of modern veterinary assistance. The daughter who acts as a subsidiary nurse attached to the coastguard station has been made pregnant by Harris, the local schoolmaster, whose own family demand his financial support. Johnny, who seems the most normal of them, mysteriously disappears on the night when he intends to present his girlfriend Nancy M'Clurg with an expensive engagement ring. The teacher has recorded in a diary that he has grown tired of Hessie and that he suspects that the father is not quite mentally stable. The main dramatic thrust of the play is the foundering on a shoal of a ship carrying rare artefacts from an unnamed British museum to Scotland for safekeeping.

As ever with Tomelty the nautical details are authentic and there is a loving catalogue of placenames: Knockinelder, Ratalla, Corrig, Portkelly and Cannon Rock, that was a feature of his later work. Things begin to go wrong when Sam finds a small coffin-shaped box floating in from the wreck and decides that its contents, some bones dressed with gold ornaments, have supernatural powers to grant requests and, to the dismay of his wife Sebina, seems prepared to worship it. His requests are not extravagant: to dry out the bog in the jib-field, to stop the Kerry cow from wandering; instead of a few 'paltry acres' he'll make 'the farm of Sam Sirk like the Garden of Eden'. The Sirk family household is subject to a number of unnerving events that cause Sebina to hit her obeisant husband with a poker, leaving him for dead. All of the peculiarities are logically explained, the leaching of the bog, the disappearance of Johnny, even the mysterious death of the prize black pig that Sam and Dendy Dale regard as unlucky. Sam, traumatised by the blow to his skull, reverts to a past event in which he relives the drowning of his brother Billy, approximately proving Harris's speculation about latent madness in the Sirk family.

As noted earlier, in a reminiscence about World War II published by the *Honest Ulsterman* in 1989, the poet Roy McFadden remembers Sam Hanna Bell announcing: 'Joe has been reading Chekhov.' To judge by the play's literally explosive ending, when delayed-action bombs start going off, possibly killing Harris, it seemed that Joe had been reading Shaw as well. The ending, whether consciously or not, owes something to *Heartbreak House* (1919) and leaves a number of issues unresolved, including Sam's mental health and Hessie's pregnancy. This sense of life's continuing willy-nilly is quite characteristic of Tomelty's dramaturgy and it is not necessarily a fault. In one speech towards the end of Act III the author, in the voice of Hessie objecting to her stern mother's use of the word 'heathen' to describe her poor addled husband, outlines his evolving moral world:

> Heathen, heathen – that's all you ever want to talk about. It's a wonder the word doesn't choke you, you use it that often. You were afraid of what God might do. God wouldn't do anything to that helpless soul. The God that you worship isn't a god at all – he's a monster.

By now it was clear that Tomelty had assembled a number of themes, preoccupations and techniques that formed his literary and critical world; to use a metaphor appropriate to his older skills, the palette from which he generated his portrait of the world was wide and nearly complete. Certain themes, noted already, continued to absorb him: madness (both the gentle and the violent), poverty, the nature of the Northern Ireland state, religion and belief with particular reference to the priestly vocation, the unforgivable bullying of the weak, life in working-class Belfast and that of the people who had to wrest a living from poor land and the wayward sea and, of course, love and sexual attraction. *Poor Errand*, which was first performed on 5 April 1943, is a remarkable example of how earlier themes and characters can be anatomised and reassembled to create a finer piece of work. The title comes from the disparaging Ulster reaction to a wilful or pointless action and interestingly uses the Belfast Blitz of the spring of 1941 as a dramatic element in the story. An authentic ironical touch appears in the first act when Stephen Durnan, the protagonist, says: 'I don't think we'll ever get air raids here.'

It is set in the city in a working-class area but its chief character is from the country. Durnan is a deckhand turned docker who has just come to live with his sluttish wife Winnie in a shared house. He is kind, intelligent, conscious of his lack of formal education and having about him an air of unrest. As such it was an ideal part for Tomelty. He makes friends with Becky Mitchell, a next-door neighbour, older than he but, unlike Winnie, well groomed and thus an object of suspicion and slander in the street. As she puts it: 'I think it's better to dye hair than to have it dirty and grey. And paint the nails rather than have them fringed in mourning.' (Dirty fingernails were one of the author's pet hates).

The problem with reading a play rather than being present at a performance is that the surge and truth of the dramatic action are missing and some of the characterisation supplied by a skilled actor can seem webby when read cold in print. The character of

Becky seems almost too good to be true. Not only is she free from the meanness that characterises Winnie and Stephen's landlord Stoupe, but she is endowed with remarkable powers like Cinderella's fairy godmother, on first-name terms with many professional men in the city from her days as a super-barmaid in the Romeo and Juliet.

It is gradually revealed that the cause of Durnan's brooding is that he killed his wife's father, a sea captain, because he holds him responsible for the deaths of two of his brothers and several friends through maritime malpractice. He had married Winnie in a kind of compensatory gesture but they have nothing in common. She is from the city (with several threatening brothers) while he longs to retire home to the country to the 'Isle o'Corr'. Injured at work, he hopes with the compensation payment to return: 'We could buy a small place of our own. Have a couple of calves, one or two pigs and a few fowl.' The vengeful Winnie reports him to the insurance company as a malingerer and in a rage, after he has revealed that he killed her father, he silences her too. Almost immobile with fear and hate (reading Dostoyevsky for solace), he is persuaded by Becky to report Winnie's death as resulting from the air raid with which the play concludes. The dubious morality of the deception seems more bald in print than during the stage action and there is not much doubt that the audiences approved of the shift.

The play shows a nice balance of urban and rural values and is very much of its time. The implicit sexual affair between Stoupe and Winnie is expressed euphemistically to suit the mores of the day as 'taking her to the pictures' (to Durnan's obvious unconcern) and Stoupe, before he leaves to join the RAF, sells 'the key' (right to tenancy) and the furniture to a future tenant even though it was obtained through hire-purchase. What is interesting to the reader is how, taking the elements of the venal bullying captain, the austere unforgiving Durnan and his unwholesome wife, while retaining their names, Tomelty built them into a more coherent structure in the novel *Red is the Port Light* five years later.

8

Right Again, Barnum

AS ITS TITLE IMPLIES, THIS IS a sequel to the *Barnum* play discussed in an earlier chapter. It was first performed in the Group on 7 December 1943, with Min Milligan as Martha Marley, the same character that she played in *Barnum Was Right* and with James Young, as Willie John, the first openly gay character on the Ulster stage. What was hinted at in the ur-*Barnum* was made manifest here and became even more blatant when in *Mugs and Money* Gugs says about him without either malice or concern, 'You'd rather have the Navy.'

It is Spring 1941. Belfast is surviving the Luftwaffe Blitz – just. On Easter Tuesday at least 900 people were killed and 1,500 seriously injured in the worst single air raid of the war on any city outside London. Security services were grossly inadequate and many thousands tried to leave the city. The stations of Dundalk, Drogheda and Dublin on the Great Northern Railway became crowded with refugees, one a bewildered Air Raid Warden in full gear with steel helmet. Local social services did what they could to alleviate the great distress and many Belfast people had their first experience of the 'Free State'. Tomelty had experienced that raid at first hand and had written eloquently about it for the *Irish Times* on 19 April 1941. He was still living in 95 Dover Street in the part of the city that suffered saturation bombing. He described standing at the door when on a night brightly lit by a three-quarter moon, the sirens went and the alert was, as so often in the past, barely heeded. Then he heard the noise of a plane 'high-up':

> Then suddenly to the north of the city wee lights began to fall from the sky. They were small like the lights you'd see on a child's Christmas tree but as they floated down they became brighter and brighter. I hurried into the middle of the road fascinated by them. There was a sort of magnesium brightness about them. They made the moon look dull – like a slice of turnip.

He describes the tails of his coat being lifted over his shoulders by a blast while the maid was covered in soot from head to foot. Venturing out again into the Falls Road he could see evidence of devastation while the Air Raid Wardens listed the names of the streets that had been flattened, as the little jerry-built red-brick houses collapsed like rows of dominoes.

> And so the night went on and the dawn crept over a pink sky. I don't think any of us noticed the dawn – for in a sense it had never been night.

When that Wednesday dawned he realised that he was still standing in the doorway, not having moved for four or five hours. He picked his way through the debris to the Falls Swimming Baths, noting that many once over-populated streets had been annihilated. The baths had been drained to accommodate some of the dead bodies, continually sprayed with pungent disinfectant, that could not be displayed for identification in the Markets:

> Bodies of the poor, they were, of the homeless poor, lying in their own shabby blankets. You only had to look at the blankets to know that – blankets that had known the rough face of the washboard for years, blankets that were thin and devoid of fleece.

The piece finished with the sentence: 'Tonight the sky is clear and the stars are bright. But you look twice at them now – just to make sure.' The Luftwaffe returned on 4 May, having realised that what Martha Marley called 'insanitary' bombs did more tactical damage than the heavy-explosive bombs (HEs). The Great Fire of Belfast did much more material destruction but caused only a fifth of the casualties, largely because the inhabitants, with no trust in the noisome street shelters, had begun the practice of 'ditching', setting up bivouacs on the surrounding hills for the hours of darkness, continuing for months until it was felt that the danger was past. In fact *Operation Barbarossa*, Hitler's repetition of Napoleon's titanic error in attacking Russia, meant that the Wehrmacht and the Luftwaffe were ordered east. The entry into the war by America after the Japanese attack on Pearl Harbor and the defeat of the Afrika Korps at El Alamein had essentially turned the tide. Belfast would see no more raids.

By the time of the opening night of *Right Again, Barnum*, two and a half years afterwards, the war had left the cities and would not return again until its last year when the V1 and V2 rockets hammered southeast England. By then Belfast was definitely out of range. The Blitz was no longer a painful subject and the play was a kind of exorcism by which the comic aspects of the evacuation might be used for further therapeutic comedy. The egregious Marleys – Rabby, the feckless sentimental sash-carrying Hibernian; Barney Brudge, his Orange buddy going through yet another period of religious fervour, during which he wildly mis-cites a stream of dodgy Biblical texts; Rabby's gullible daughter Gugs and his gay son Willie John (referred to in those years as a 'jenny-joe') and the materfamilias, Martha, ill-educated, tolerant and full of optimistic energy, the part played by Tomelty's mother-in-law, Min Milligan – they were a ready-made comic troupe and available again for comic exploitation. They provided a blueprint that would later be applied to *The McCooeys*.

The essential optimistic gullibility of the working-class family is undoubtedly comic; *The End House*, seen as a kind of serious application of Marleyism, proved to be too dark, too pessimistic, to cheer up a wartime audience. Nearly everyone could identify with the beset family, sustained by their wits, minimal state welfare and a baseless Micawberism, waiting for the bit of luck that will end their stressful poverty. The nature of the characters and their sudden necessary exile opened the door to, on the whole, genial comedy situations and a dollop of farce that the author cleverly exploits. The plot is more contrived and less realistic than in the earlier play. The element of suckerdom again involves the gullible Gugs who believes that the smooth-talking Jack Hart is sincere in his courtship and amorous declarations. He appears at the station and conveys the Marleys to a country cottage where they may have shelter and they assume that he is the owner, especially when he continues to be helpful. As Gugs approvingly remarks: 'It would put ye in mind of the story of the Good Samaritan.' Yet he is so obviously untrustworthy for all his charm that only members of the audience as innocent and traumatised as the Marleys could fail to see that he is a conman.

He pretends to be an archaeologist trying to assemble, he claims, the bones of William III's white horse on which he crossed the nearby Boyne – that firmly-held belief incorporated on many an Orange banner. In fact the horse was sorrel in colour and there was never any need for the Dutch king to cross the river in that indecisive battle. It is the kind of tale that might convince Ulster people but in fact is a mere piece of instinctive kite-flying by a practised crook. In reality northern politics play little if any part in the play, except for the fact that Martha and most of the characters are Protestant and Orange, while Rabby is a sash-wearing member of the Ancient Order of Hibernians. Like the inclusion of a gay man as one of the characters, it was quite a daring idea and unusual at the time. It was typical of Tomelty, who loathed any form of sectarianism, to face the defining fact of Belfast life more safely in a comedy. In fact, because of the greater stress of the war and the unselective horror of the Blitz, it was a time of less virulent tribal fear and hate than in the decades before and after.

Hart is in fact a smuggler with an instinct for dodgy deals. The King Billy horse caper is only one of a number of scams that he is considering. When he hears that some musical scores that belonged to Albert Bonein, an old neighbour who used to play the cornet at street corners, have been preserved and are in the cottage, he senses another opportunity. They had been commandeered by Willie John on the presumption of the old man's death and now, it seems, could be valuable. Hart's wooing of Gugs is, of course, a mere ploy to get access to the music scores that prove to be worthless, as Bonein, who had not died, makes clear. All the best-laid schemes go astray and the play ends in farcical confusion.

It was intended as a comedy and, in spite of being a sequel, worked well. The exodus from the beleaguered city allowed the author to assemble many of the characters who had made *Barnum Was Right* so successful. As ever, characterisation and excellent acting carried the day with, as well as Min Milligan, such Group stalwarts as Elizabeth Begley as Gugs and James Young as her brother. As with Sean O'Casey's *Juno and the Paycock*, two different plays, one a tragedy, the other near farce, are welded together with a certain clumsiness. The maunderings of Captain Boyle and Joxer, though brilliantly written and the more popular element of the play, seem hardly to connect with the sorrows of Juno, her pregnant daughter Mary and her executed son Johnny. I make no comparison other than structural: the comic 'turns' of Rabby, his crony Barney Brudge and his wife Martha are treated almost as detachable items of a variety concert, as when Juno and Mary are made to sing 'Home to Our Mountains' from Act IV of Verdi's *Il Trovatore*. Their purpose is to keep up the interest of the audience while the main plot, the finally unsuccessful sale of the 'valuable' music manuscripts, the jilting of Gugs and the disappearance of Hart, comes to its predictable conclusion.

There is plenty of broad local comedy and some accurately zeroed darts based on the underlying darkness of the perennial Northern Ireland situation, as in Martha Marley's commonsense comment:

> To tell the truth we never thought that much about religion to fight over it. When you're on the dole year in and year out you have enough to worry you.

The script is peppered with knowing, deliberately inserted remarks to please the punters, while their speakers remain in character: Martha dismissing Barney Brudge's religious fervour: 'If you feel like preaching why don't ye do it in Belfast where they need it?'; the gulf between town and gown neatly expressed by Barney: 'What would the Queen's University men know about King William's horse? I doubt if there's one Orangeman in the whole building.' One speech reflects the low level of labour relations in the Belfast plane factory during the war. Gugs, seriously attracted to Hart, offers to supply him with an appropriate gift: 'I know a foreman in Short and Harland's. I'll get him to make you a cigarette-lighter.' The current urban legend had it that a visiting dignitary from London had been greatly impressed when a workman had boasted he had made a hundred lighters during the previous week, thinking he had said 'fighters'.

The play was intended as the lightest of comedy and succeeded as such, the ambient jokes intended to maintain the pantomime atmosphere of a Christmas show. The farcical elements were not overdone; Rabby is forced by his wife to wear the corsets he is smuggling to Liza Lowry and comes to grief when he mistakenly boards the train for Dublin rather than Belfast, but the gag is not over-milked. The quick *volte-face* when a supposed picture of Martin Luther in which Martha Marley discerns 'something saintly about him. Wouldn't ye know he had a message to deliver?' turns out to be one of Gladstone is neatly done:

> God forgimme, but there's something evil about his eyes. Sir
> Edward Carson put an end to his carry on. Only for Sir Edward
> we might have all been in the Free State the day.

Proper timing by Min Milligan must have made that seriously-intended line extremely funny, since that is precisely where she is at that moment. The author's light touch here and elsewhere portrayed enabled him to write excellent comedy that was rooted in reality. He was then free to write about the city and province he knew with affection but also with a clear-eyed vision of the place, warts and all. He believed that no matter how unpretentious, or escapist, a play, it couldn't help but reveal, admittedly indirectly, the assumptions and values of its time. If this detail is too elaborate it tends to date the play, however interesting it might be to the historian. For example Martha's surprise and disapproval at seeing the refugee Gugs wearing slacks would strike the 90 per cent-trousered audiences of today as meaningless. Then it took courage to have a gay man, unselfconsciously camp, hoping for the settlement of a damages suit because his hair was frazzled by being kept too long under the heaters in a salon. The hairdresser was too busy 'behind the dure kissing and slabbering a peeler'. With the money he would open a dance club, a feature of the Belfast social life of the time:

> A small place, ma, with hidden lights and the walls blue and one
> or two palms in flowerpots. I'd call it 'Tahiti' and have it
> respectable – ye know, Ma, like Fruit Hill. And you could come
> and look after the cloakroom and mabbe sell minerals ... And I
> could get me Da a royal blue uniform and have a wee palm
> sticking from his cap, and he could do commissionaire outside,
> to see that no riff-raff got in.

An actor of James Young's sensibility could make that dream seem poignant rather than tacky.

The character of Martha, the Orangewoman who married a Catholic, was quite a departure in the play-safe culture of the

UGT of the time. Tomelty wrote it with his future mother-in-law in mind for the part. He was keen to emphsise Martha's industry, strength and patience with a dysfunctional husband. A complimentary phrase of the time was that a tidied room or litter-free yard was 'a bit more Protestant-looking'. Endemic ignorance of the other tribe's mores did not preclude due praise. Though Tomelty's professional life as a painter was spent mainly in the Catholic/nationalist enclave of the lower Falls Road, an innate lack of suspicion and intense curiosity led to a wide acquaintance with 'the other sort'. The politics- religion- and ideology-free *McCooeys* was not, however, so rendered through cowardice or instruction from above but with the conviction that these measures were essentially superficial; 'the colonel's lady and Judy O'Grady were sisters under the skin' and both sides of the house shared the same joys, hopes, sorrows – and survival techniques. Martha, busily falsifying her claim for loss of property, cries: 'I'm in a creative mood the day.'

As the porter of a bank, Rabby is required to wear a tall silk hat and it was one of the items he made sure of saving during the Easter week air raid. He and Martha, who incessantly calls him 'Towser', are in essence an appliqué knockabout music-hall duo with the immemorial elements of farce written for them, including sausages, corsets and loss of trousers. Rabby's sidekick and 'booze-'em' companion Barney Brudge, the drink-addicted schizophrenic and unreliable decorator, who, when drunk, suddenly becomes a Bible-misquoting preacher against the evils of alcohol, serves little plot purpose but is included as a foil for the Marleys. He represents, too, in a mild and here comical way, another example of Tomelty's deep interest in mental imbalance. He tries, of course, to involve himself in the 'bones' scam with Hart, suggesting that in parts of the country where William III had less than iconic status they could be passed off as those of Finn MacCool, whom Barney, less than competent in the facts of Irish history, believes was one of the United Irishmen who fought against Oliver

Cromwell. Tomelty's characters were often given odd names: 'Aneas' in *The Singing Bird* (and not spelled as in Virgil); Wallace MacAstocker in *The End House* (a distinctly odd name for a Belfast Taig) and Albert Bonein in the two *Barnum*s. This slight eccentricity was a kind of hallmark; he collected slightly odd names much as Dickens did but he could devise nonce words as he needed them: the name of the second-hand clothes dealer, Henrietta Toosel, in *The McCooeys*, played by Elizabeth Begley, was constructed from 'to' and 'sell'. The surname Marley, though not unknown in Belfast – there is a street song called 'Mickey Marley's Roundabout' – could have had its origin in the usual street name for the game of marbles and the gibe: 'Yer head's a marley.'

Tomelty was adept at appropriate comic lines: Rabby counters Martha's unease at being in County Louth with 'Well, you're in it [the Free State] now and damn glad of it!' Other topical laughs would have come from: 'You couldn't get walking in Drogheda. It's like the retreat from Moscow'; 'I've been travelling all day like an Israelite'; ' … you'll come no Gandhi stuff here' and ' … Willie John has wrote a fugue'.

The play ends in disappointment for all; even the slight chicanery that nets Rabby £20 when he pawns Hart's smuggled rings is ultimately unprofitable. (The purchasing power of that amount of money by today's standards would be well over £700). The note placed in his boot for safety is irretrievable because, as Martha shouts before she rushes at him, 'He's walked the money into pulp!' As the Christmas offering for a Belfast still bearing the scars of its Blitz, it was inevitably popular. Like most sequels it had not the bite or the insouciance of the original but it provided an escapist evening's entertainment. The advantage had swung to the side of the Allies and detailed preparations were underway for the invasion of Europe, the now proverbial 'D-Day' of 6 June 1944 that would happen exactly 182 days later. There was no need for any explanation in the text as to the significance of the title; it was explained in the last act of *Barnum Was Right* and would reappear in its later incarnation, *Mugs and Money*.

Tomelty, in his treatment of his characters, never showed the least hint of condescension. He guyed them for their pretensions, misapprehensions and gullibility but his admiration for the heroic virtues shows clear. They were resilient, incredibly cheerful and resourceful, innately kind and, though instinctively sectarian in self-defence, they took individuals as they found them, irrespective of class or creed. He knew this because he had become one of them, sharing their sorrows and rarer joys. When the play opened, the Beveridge Report, the blueprint for the coming Welfare State, was one year old and some alleviation of the conditions of working-class and unemployed people had become a possibility. Implicit in the play was the author's admiration for the courage of the people of the blitzed city. In its light-hearted treatment and optimistic tenor it was an oblique tribute to their resourcefulness.

9

Odd Man Out

I N 1945 F.L. GREEN (1902–1953), an English writer who settled in Belfast in his thirties, published a novel, *Odd Man Out*. It tells of the aftermath of an IRA raid in which Johnny McQueen, the leader of the gang, played in the film version by James Mason (1909–84), is wounded and charts his semi-delirious, nightmarish progress through the wintry city hoping to reach the docks and safety. It came to the attention of Carol Reed (1906–76), whose reputation as a film director had steadily grown during the war, especially with the army film, *The Way Ahead* (1944), that told the story of how a bunch of conscripts were moulded into a fighting unit. He saw the potential for a superior film in Green's novel and had him prepare a screenplay that was further worked on by R.C. Sherriff (1896–1975) who was the author of *Journey's End* (1925), one of the most famous of the plays about the Great War. His play, *Home Before Seven* (1950), would become another hit twenty-five years after the first and one of the offerings of the UGT.

Reed had come upon the book almost by accident. As the story goes, he was driving along the Bayswater Road in London and was halted by a traffic light stuck on red. Visibly impatient, he was handed a copy of the novel by his front-seat passenger. He had just sufficient time to read the first page before he could move off again but it was time enough for him to be captivated by the story. A similar lucky coincidence brought the novel *December Bride*, to the screen in 1991. Written by Tomelty's friend Sam Hanna Bell in 1951, it was reprinted several times by Blackstaff Press, in 1982 with a cover by Sir William Orpen (1878–1931) called *The Wash House* (1905). One of the editors of a Regent Street film company called Little Bird had to go on a longish train journey and called at Hatchard's in Piccadilly to look for something to read. She was attracted by the cover and when she returned to London on the Monday, she was full of the book's film potential.

Reed needed star names to sell his film but he also needed authentic Irish voices for the secondary characters. It was Mason's twenty-eighth film of well over a hundred. His Irish accent was quite good – he had had a season at the Gate Theatre in Dublin with Micheál Mac Liammóir and Hilton Edwards in his twenties before becoming the lead in many British 'quota quickies'. During the mid-1940s, in a series of films, notably *The Man in Grey* (1943), *The Seventh Veil* (1945) and *The Wicked Lady* (1946), he became the leading British star. In these he was cruel, saturnine and irresistible to the women whom he treated so badly – and to the cinema audiences of the time. In *Odd Man Out*, in his portrayal of the activist with doubts, the slightly husky voice that female fans found so attractive becomes even more engrossing as his physical condition worsens. It showed a capacity for pathos and subtlety that was not required for the 'man-you-love-to-hate' parts.

From the wide pool of established British actors Reed cast Fay Compton as a reluctant helper, Elwyn Brook-Jones as a struck-off doctor who patches up Mason's wounds and Robert Newton, whose eye-rolling, bravura style made him a splendid Long John Silver in *Treasure Island* (1950), but was in danger of tearing the fabric of the film with his performance as Lukey, an unsuccessful artist, who hopes to 'paint the soul' of the dying man. In McQueen's gang the only non-Irish actor, apart from Mason himself, was the Canadian, Robert Beatty, whose native accent was remarkably close to that of middle-class Belfast anyway. The Irish actors were drawn mainly from the Abbey and the Gate, the former supplying one of the original pre-Abbey Dublin actors, W.G. Fay as Fr Tom and the great star of the Abbey realist period, F.J. McCormick (the stage name of Peter Judge) who played Shell, the bird fancier who later betrays McQueen to the police. Other Abbey actors were Maureen Delaney as the treacherous landlady, Theresa O'Brien, Harry Hutchinson as the waiter in the Crown Bar and Denis O'Dea as a driven but honourable RUC head constable who is McQueen's nemesis. Other members of the pool of talented Irish actors whose careers were greatly helped by the success of the film included Cyril Cusack, his wife Maureen Kiely, Dan O'Herlihy, Noel Purcell as the conductor of the tram, who before this had been known mainly as a pantomime dame, Wilfrid Brambell (later famous as the elder Steptoe) as a passenger in the same tram, Eddie Byrne and Kathleen Ryan as McQueen's self-sacrificing girlfriend.

There were a number of bit-parts played by British actors on screen for minutes whose careers blossomed later: Geoffrey Keen as a squaddy, who afterwards worked his way to head of Mogul Oil; William Hartnell as Fencie, the Crown barman, became the first Dr Who, and, as a girl in a telephone box, the revue star and comic actress, Dora Bryan, was to become one of Britain's best-loved screen presences. One 'local' British actor, Guy Rolfe, played the small part of an RUC constable. Very tall and a former boxer and racing car driver, he was local in the sense that he was one of the leading actors who played in repertory in the Grand Opera House in Belfast during the war. A successful film career began with Cavalcanti's *Nicholas Nickleby* (1947).

Oddly enough, since accents were paramount, the only UGT actors used were Tomelty himself, his mother-in-law and his niece, Maura Milligan, who played a little girl who, following her ball into the air raid shelter where McQueen is resting, comes face to face with the fugitive. She was taken to the location with other possible candidates but had no great expectation of success. She had neither curls nor ringlets, describing her hair as 'just sticks', as was the current description for straight hair. Reed, considering the shot, decided that he wanted a child 'just this height', holding out his hand. Maura walked underneath – and got the part and her name on the credits. In fact, Reed could see that the little girl had a remarkable face, one he knew the camera would love and enable her to steal her scene with Robert Beatty. Her strange, almost pitying look earlier at the wounded Mason in the shelter was one of the most thrilling moments in the whole film. Tomelty, credited in the main title as 'Irish advisor', played 'Gin' Jimmy into whose cab Mason is bundled kindly by Geoffrey Keen.

Dressed in a filthy sodden hat and raincoat, rain dropping from his presumptuous moustache, Tomelty dominated the screen for the short time he was in shot and his manner of fake commiseration and reassurance as he dumped Mason grotesquely on a disused hip-bath, on one of the many open spaces that were a relic of the Luftwaffe raids, was masterly. The horse-drawn cab was a piece of appliqué design. There were none such in the Belfast of the time; even the few available in Dublin were used as a tourist attraction. 'Gin' Jimmy was on screen for less than ten minutes but he made quite an impression, not only on the Belfast filmgoers who knew him from the Group, but generally, and I am convinced that his brief appearance proved to David Lean that he was an actor whom the camera might love. Many years later Roma Tomelty met Mason at a party and introduced herself. He told her he remembered her father with great affection, asked about his health and said, 'I'll never forget my Gin Jimmy.'

Tomelty played a significant part in suggesting the locations for particular shots and acted as a kind of artistic advisor as well. The use of non-studio locations was comparatively new then; *cinema-vérité* would have been regarded at best as an artistic aberration and generally as professional incompetence. Ralph Brinton, the art director, replicated the Belfast cobbled streets for the studio shots and filmed some of the night scenes in Shepperton but one of the great visceral excitements of the film is the portrayal of the bleak, grey, just post-war industrial city. It is never named but with William Alwyn's music and the magnificent black and white photography of Robert Krasker, it becomes an extra actor. From the opening aerial shot of the wintry dockland, finally zeroing in on the Albert Clock striking four, to the trajectory of a football to where it lands in the twilit back streets, there is an utterly gripping display of film photography at its finest. And then there are the air raid shelters.

These were a relic of the Second World War, representing Belfast's pitifully inadequate response to the threat of aerial bombardment by the Luftwaffe. Once it had become clear that, after the German occupation of northern France, the city was no longer out of range of the Dorniers, Junkers and Heinkels, a feverish attempt was made to build shelters. The greater part of Belfast, however, was built on a swampy subsoil called 'sleech' that made the construction of underground shelters virtually impossible. The authorities' only real alternative was to build public shelters at surface level. They were essentially rectangular boxes constructed of red brick (Belfast's favourite material) strengthened with steel rods. To say they were unsightly would be a considerable understatement and, since they were built largely on narrow backstreets, were an inevitable traffic hazard, this mitigated by the fact that because of the unavailability of petrol to all but 'essential' users, there wasn't much traffic. Slatted doors, locked at first, tended to disappear when the summer bonfire season began. Some still had seats, also latticed, round the walls and were often resorted to by lovers and, less wholesomely, by people *in extremis*.

Brinton decided that the shelter in which McQueen should take refuge should have graffiti added for greater authenticity and had 'Mary loves Brian' chalked on the wall. Tomelty demurred and Brinton handed him the chalk and was totally confused when he wrote: 'No Surrender – Remember 1690'. 'What,' Brinton asked, 'has 1690 to do with it?' Tomelty replied with a smile: 'Ah, it's all tied up with William III.' Brinton reacted with all of an Englishman's certainty that he was being made fun of by an Irishman, whose wicked sense of humour had already been demonstrated several times. Tomelty did not argue and said: 'Scrub it – scrub it!' Brinton allowed him to continue: 'If it's important keep it; if it's atmospheric.' The anecdote was printed in a profile of Tomelty by his friend Sam Hanna Bell in the *Ulster Tatler* and it finished with a tailpiece that confirmed the appropriateness of Tomelty's idea. Years afterwards he met a man who had seen *Odd Man Out* on an Atlantic voyage on the *Queen Mary*. 'Mr Tomelty,' he said, 'when I saw those words chalked up, it took me right back to Dee Street!' Another aspect to the story, not adverted to by Bell, is the readiness with which strangers approached Tomelty conversationally and how readily they were received.

The winter of 1947 was bitterly cold with a prolonged near-Arctic spell. Trains were stopped by banked-up snow, roads were impassable and coal, effectively the only fuel, all but impossible to move from the pitheads. Belfast, dependent on its colliers, was often a freezing place. The lined oilskins supplied to Tomelty as a member of the film crew on location were afterwards adapted by her mother as a rain cape for daughter Roma. One bitingly cold night, during one of the constant delays that are such a part of filming, while Reed was lining up a shot in Boomer Street, one of countless Falls Road side streets that disappeared after urban renewal, Tomelty went to a local chippie for a fish supper (costing four old pence in those pre-inflationary days). Tomelty described the incident in an interview for the *Belfast Telegraph* in their daily diary 'An Ulster Log' on Wednesday, 28 April 1976. Reed had died three days earlier.

> Older folk will remember it in the film as the street with the stairs. I wasn't in the scene and I had gone round the corner to Jo Raffo's café for a fish supper. I was standing eating it and I asked Reed if he would like one too. He said he would, so I went and got three more, one for him, one for the cameraman and another one for myself. The three suppers cost a bob and Sir Carol complained that I hadn't put enough vinegar on his. The funny thing was that just a night or two previous he had been sitting down to a 17-course banquet in the Savoy Hotel, London. And here he was eating a 4d supper on the Falls Road. I thought, you know, how democratic.

In the same interview Tomelty revealed that he was hired as a 'local colour' advisor for the film at a retainer of £25 a week, which then had a buying power of £726 in today's money. Owing to strict union rules forbidding dual employment in a film, his name as expert was given as Jose Tomelty. He mentioned Reed's intense professional curiosity:

> He wanted to know all sorts of things like where you would post a letter at the City Hall and the sort of uniform the warders in Crumlin Road jail wore ... We never thought it was going to be such an important picture. But I have been told many times by people who know films that it was Reed's masterpiece. I was very sorry to hear of his death. He was a real gentleman and a great director. He understood the actor.

The film ends with the death of McQueen and his sweetheart Kathleen on the docks, as the ship that might have been his escape route sails out of the harbour. Green's novel ends more realistically with Kathleen shooting Johnny and then shooting herself to prevent his return to jail and inevitable capital punishment. The box office advisors warned against so nihilistic a conclusion to the film as bad for business. Instead she fires the two shots that give the police the legal right to return fire as the constable, played by Eddie Byrne, explains to his chief. The last shot pans to the Albert Clock again, telling the chimes of midnight, almost obscured by the blinding snow.

10
Red is the Port Light

NINETEEN FORTY-EIGHT WAS A YEAR OF remarkable literary activity: it saw the production of the play *All Souls' Night*, the writing of *The Singing Bird*, the initial work on *The McCooeys* and Tomelty's first novel, *Red is the Port Light*. Apart from all other considerations the book is a loving portrait of Strangford Lough, its coastal villages and its people. The large, almost landlocked, sea-lough is strikingly beautiful, speckled with islands but with an extraordinarily strong tidal race at its southern end at the tip of the long finger of the Ards Peninsula between Portaferry and the village of Strangford. Tomelty observes his characters and their environment with a painter's eye:

> The fields slid gently down and the rows of hawthorns seemed to peg them lest they should slide into the sea.

James Joyce once boasted that if some disaster had erased the centre of Edwardian Dublin it could be replicated accurately from *Ulysses*. To a lesser extent a blueprint for Portaferry in the early decades of the twentieth century may be found in this novel:

> On one side of the road the little houses rested shoulder to shoulder. They were barn shaped, and sparrows and blue tits flitted about the moss margins of the blue slates.
>
> There were straws and streaks of droppings about the eaves, marking where the sandmartins had nested earlier in the year. Durnan's eyes caught the crooked windows, and he glanced at the old women stretching their heads coaxingly to the light, stitching rapidly the flowers on the linen handkerchiefs that brought them their bread; stitching with their mouths mumping, eager to finish a cloth before darkness came.
>
> Passing the house of a bachelor he could see, on the flat window sills, newly tarred bladders, pieces of burnt cork and sail needles with slanting eyes that gaped like the mouths of goldfish.
>
> The white road was swept dry by the October wind and its face was crisp. In the opening where the small slip started he saw empty limpet shells and lifeless starfish. On the other side of the road was the wall that kept the sea from washing over the doorsteps of the villagers, and beyond it was the sea ... The row of houses finished with a gable resting against a mass of stones that reached to its chimney; it was the end of the main street of Portaferry ... Some day, he thought, the water licking and seeping under the muddy road would topple them into the sea. This had always been one of his nightmares; these banks crashing down on top of him.

It was, then, a village tormented by the sea and many of its people, like those in the other settlements along the coast, depended upon it for livelihood and treated it with a mixture of wariness and respect. Catholic and Protestant in a small mixed community such as Portaferry were more obviously mutually interdependent and Tomelty felt by instinct that such was the only real and lasting basis of amity. He was dismissive of sentimental bromides, preferring the demands of necessity to any appeal to brotherhood. The old couple, Robert and Susan King, stand as an example of love and common sense overcoming atavism. One aspect of village life, the relationship between priest and flock, he portrays in what is almost a cliché of Irish drama: the canon is older and wiser and more tolerant than the brusque, self-centred curate. It was the theme of *The White Steed* (1939) by Paul Vincent Carroll (1900–68), a playwright from the next county, Louth, and earned him the reputation of being anti-clerical. Perhaps Tomelty's intention was simply to ask the young for more forbearance with the old. The young doctor who attempts to bully the ailing Susan into hospital in Newtownards is made to show less than professional tact in handling the situation. He seems not to understand the instinctive shame and terror of the workhouse or a 'home' rooted in a woman of Susan King's age, class and time:

> It isn't the poor house but a first-class hospital, where she'll get first-class treatment. Good God, man, you can't leave her down there. Why there's neither sanitary arrangements nor anything else. It's my duty to have her removed to hospital, otherwise I won't attend her. In view of that I'll lodge a complaint with the Local Authorities. Ignorant prejudices are things I won't tolerate. Either she gets out of there or I'm forced to get her out ...

A similar dislike of the bullying of the weak surfaces in the opening pages of Tomelty's other novel, *The Apprentice* (1953), when the hapless stammering undersized Francis Price is humiliated by his sneering teacher on his last day at school, though the author reserves the right to humiliate him (in the reader's eyes): 'He laughed but closed his mouth suddenly as his false teeth dropped.' Tomelty's only real show of unauthorial impatience is to be found in a meditation, as it proves ironical, on the eve of his wedding, by the novel's hero, Stephen Durnan:

> This really was life. Not an abundance of it but enough of it to show him that he lived almost like a human animal. People like

his mother never found out much about life. They never troubled
to find out about it. Things came to them and they never
questioned from where or why. That was the curse of the poor,
this stupid fatalism. They took no action or say in the making of
their own lives. Everything was directed by God. God's will was
strong and there was no moving against it. If God willed they
lived in poverty, they did so. If God willed they should be dirty
they made no effort to clean themselves.

These musings lead eventually and not unexpectedly to a ritual
cleansing, with a twinge of dramatic irony at the end:

> Now everything about him was spotless, and a great heat filled
> his body. Outside the rain was falling and when he opened the
> door the breeze blew some on his chest. He moved out until the
> rain peppered his body, keeping his hand on the latch, lest Robert
> should come out, and on finding him standing naked in the rain,
> might think he had taken leave of his senses.

But the most obvious physical force in the novel is the ever-
present, inescapable sea. As indicated earlier, Tomelty himself
had never been a sailor but with uncles and cousins wedded to
the sea and a centuries-old family involvement in the Portaferry–
Strangford ferry, he could call on what Irish folklorists call
béaloideas ('oral tradition'). With his rapid intelligence and
imaginative empathy, his awareness of the mariners' lives, the
conditions under which they then worked, the best way of storing
cargo in a hold, the behaviour of a ship in a storm, with special
emphasis on the behaviour of deck cargo during a squall, the
blessed relief of a safe landfall, the urge to return in spite of known
hazard – all of these he experienced by a kind of artistic osmosis.
He could enter the imaginative life of the seaman and replicate it
accurately without actually experiencing it. Long nights spent
listening to his Uncle Patrick's stories of voyages, both local and
deep-sea, the former not necessarily less dangerous than the latter,
had given him all the experience his lively creative imagination
and his preternaturally observant eye needed for his purpose. Just

as Shakespeare seemed to know the exact nature of the life of courtier, soldier, lawyer, schoolmaster, poet, peasant – and sailor, without necessarily having been any of these, so Tomelty the writer could recreate accurately the essence without getting his feet wet.

He was not afraid of the sea, preferring to make his many, necessary journeys to what he would never have called the mainland by sea rather than by plane. He probably subscribed to the view, rather sentimentally expressed, that he put in the mouth of old Robert King, the Protestant husband of Susan:

> You know, Stephen, at sea people don't feel the same about religion as they do on land. On land they never seem to find God, so they must fight about Him all the time. But at sea you see Him everywhere, in the water, in the moon, in the stars, and you can hear Him in the wind … He's always there like a strong but silent friend.

Durnan instinctively realises that the death of his mother can be a turning point in a previously blank life: 'He wanted a rest after tramping the seas since he was thirteen.' His childhood had been miserable, as a bastard with no known father and a mother convulsed eternally by the shame of producing a 'by-blow'. Her death, which precedes the novel's opening, offers a new beginning, one that might banish the residual guilt of his lack of mourning for his mother and for having cost Frank Norton, a previous skipper, his deep-sea ticket, when, at an enquiry after a sinking, his evidence that Norton was drunk and incapable caused him to be found guilty. These two worms continue to gnaw, their rapacity later given an extra edge by the fact that Norton was drowned during the recent storm, responsible as well for the foundering of the *Glendry* as of the wreck that lost him his ticket.

The four short chapters that describe the stowing of the *Glendry*'s cargo of potatoes, its putting to sea and the storm that overwhelms her, are written with such brio that the slow declension into madness that follows begins to seem like an anti-climax:

> The water poured into the fo'c's'le, hugging Durnan's body, lifting him off his feet. He waited, struggling to breathe, fighting the water that flooded his mouth, his ears ... Christ, would she never settle again ... ? Was this the finish? He heard a crash and he knew the desk cargo was toppling to the hold. The brown bags falling hammered in his brain. He heard someone cry, a loud cry; then it stuttered and the sucking sound of the sea continued.

The offer of the post of lamp-trimmer on board the coaster *Glendry* on the day of Durnan's mother's funeral is accepted by him without thought and even when he discovers that the master is Frank Norton, he, with characteristic stubbornness, joins the crew. The *Glendry* sinks with only two survivors, Durnan and Fenner, a young acquaintance with only three weeks' maritime experience, whose life Durnan saves. For him the red port light of the novel's title remains a kind of guiding star, an icon that has come to mean home, security, warmth and the human love denied him as a child and denied by himself as an adult:

> The port light always fascinated him. It had the warmth of a homely fire in its warm glow. He could kneel on the deck, polishing its glass, peering into its red heart. It was to him the symbol of home, of a real home, with a wife, with children.

At the height of the storm, as he struggles to keep himself and Fenner safe on the starboard lifeboat, it is the red port light that his mind fixes on as a point of concentration that brings the two of them, half-dead, to shore.

After hours of delirium he comes partially to his senses, safe in a strange bed, tended by a woman he does not know but one whose attentive care he relishes. She assumes an almost miraculous status in his mind, a kind of personification of the port light. At the beginning he is too ill to notice any strangeness on her part, conscious merely of the unobtrusive cool care. 'He thought it strange that her hands should be so beautiful and her face was plain.' As with many another patient he finds his nurse an object of intense interest and of growing sexual attraction: 'He was aware of her breasts as she sat on the bed feeding him. They were small, round and moved slowly with the movements of her body.' In full health such thoughts should have made his essentially Puritan conscience, aggravated by his illegitimacy, uneasy. Furthermore, given the mores of the period and place, any such thoughts would have been widely regarded as immoral.

When the doctor informs him that his boat was picked up on Gunn's Island – 'The *Prince Albert*, a Portavogie fishing nabby, had pulled in there for shelter, and they found you drifting in at the dawn' – his mental and physical health improve rapidly. Fenner, the young sailor for whom he has assumed responsibility, is safe and well, and life has possibilities again. Even the woman's revelation that she is Winnie Norton, the wife of the drunken captain upon whose life Durnan unwittingly left his mark, does not diminish, but rather enhances, his euphoria. She was noted among the shipping fraternity as being frigid and refusing her husband her bed, thereby increasing his personal and vocational dysfunction. None of this diminishes Durnan's growing interest in her as a person. It is as if his maimed life finds a fellow in hers. When the intensity of his feelings and her proximity is such that he kisses her, the ambivalence of her reaction confuses them both.

Tomelty gradually reveals with ever more plangent evidence that Winnie is not quite normal and, in doing so, sets himself the artistic problem of how to handle lunacy. The condition does not lend itself to rational discussion because there is little authorial control. Durnan ascribes her aberrant behaviour, mood swings, intermittent coldness and intense silences, to the trauma of her husband's death. Her unfathomable personality and her own sense of alienation as the daughter of a Belgian sailor coming from Tamarsheeland, an island in the upper lough, seem to him sufficient explanations of her otherness and at the beginning he finds it intriguing rather than dismaying. He even tolerates her refusal to accept physical and verbal caresses in public, assuming it to be modesty and shyness. It is only later that he realises her innate sexual frigidity. Their marriage service is a perfunctory affair and their first and only lovemaking brief and crude.

As mentioned earlier, Tomelty found madness a challenge worth describing. He touches on it in *The End House* (1944) and *All Souls' Night* (1948), and *The Singing Bird* (1948) has as its main character Aneas Anketelle, a loving portrayal of harmless, almost positive, lunacy. (The song, which gives that last play its title, recurs as a motif in Durnan's imagination). True madness is not really an appropriate theme for literature since there cannot be drama without the capacity of the character to make moral judgements. It is rather the fear of the possibility of madness, the glimpse of the snakepit as when King Lear on the edge cries: 'O, let me not be mad, not mad, sweet heaven,' that provides the thrill and the suspense. It is Tomelty's portrayal of that dread possibility that shows best the effectiveness and control of his writing. The narrowness and meanness disguised as thrift that characterise Kathrine Quinn in *All Souls' Night* and Miss Price, Frankie's ghastly aunt in *The Apprentice*, are taken to such excess that there is no other word to describe their mental condition. The slow release of evidence of mental instability in *Red is the Port Light* builds up to such a climax that the final sight of Winnie, her mouth stained with grass and dandelions, swinging an open razor, is quite shocking: ' … her hand came down quickly and the razor cut his chin'. It is then that Durnan's own neurosis surfaces and his self-defence turns to blind fury and the throttling of the poor demented creature. The remaining twenty-three pages of the novel describe his own headlong descent as he tries to dispose of the body, until he too, by the end, has lost his reason:

> He could see Winnie, seeing his hands about her neck, and her
> swollen stomach. Then he saw her sprawling in the water like a

frog. Then all went black and his eyes were burning into red bulbs, a huge port light was coming to meet him. Then he fell limp on the floor. He couldn't hear Sina calling out to her daughters to go to the corner and fetch the men, as Stephen Durnan was acting like a madman.

One of the ominous signs of Winnie's degeneration was her rejection of Durnan's hospitable sharing of his cottage with the Kings when the *Summer Breeze*, the beached ketch that was their home, proves no longer habitable. Their mutual affection acts as a control system of how normal loving people have learned to live in reasonable harmony in spite of privation. They act as a counterbalance to the dysfunction of Stephen and Winnie – the ultimate assertion of the author's belief in the essential humanity of humans. Dark though the novel is, its outlook is not at all nihilistic. The rich array of characters, good, bad and different, is proof of an essentially optimistic view of life. One remembers the pleasure of good writing and the piquancy of the dialect words that place it in its parish and universe. Somehow the standard dictionary replacement words for 'nabby' (fishing smack), 'whaup' (curlew), 'lythe' (pollack) and 'loanen' (lane) seem inadequate. Tomelty's metaphors are rich and startlingly appropriate. At Durnan's mother's funeral, the clay bleeds 'its brown blood over the breastplate ... and as the grave was filled, each spadeful kissed until all melted together'; 'a powder puff lay slightly curled, like a biscuit softened with tea.'; a hair plucked from a hairbrush is 'silver like a thread of frozen rain'; pension books are wrapped 'in brown paper that looked soft and silken from usage'.

The novel as a whole was a considerable achievement done with the reassuring confidence of a wordsmith at the height of his power. His portrayal of true madness, always tricky, was brought off with skill and conviction. The book's deliberate siting in a local landscape did not diminish its universal application. Its dark matter was generated out of its author's own concomitant darkness, appearing virtually simultaneously with the staging of *All Souls'*

Night, its Strangford sibling. The structural symmetry of the novel may be slightly askew and the relationship with Fenner not fully developed, but because of its language, its drama, its wisdom and the rendering of its setting, *Red is the Port Light* must take its secure place in the canon of twentieth-century Irish literature.

11

The Dark Plays

TOMELTY'S FIRST SERIOUS DRAMA, *THE END House*, finally opened in the Abbey Theatre on 28 August 1944, with F.J. McCormick, the original Joxer in *Juno and the Paycock*, as Wallace MacAstocker. It had been completed by the author by 1938 and the notes for direction published with the playscript indicate that the setting is: 'Belfast, eighteen months before the Second World War'. Though an obvious mark for the Group it was decided by the management that it was too controversial and indeed did not get its Ulster premiere until 1994 when the Centre Stage Theatre Company staged it. As we have seen earlier, because of certain resemblances – and even debt – to the O'Casey play, the Dublin audiences tended to regard it as a comedy. Wallace, the father of the oddly-named MacAstocker family, is a man of some slight education and grandiloquent dreams; his wife, Sar Alice, does her best to keep the family together in spite of extreme poverty, a daughter with social ambitions and a paucity of common sense, and a son filled with the pathological exaltation of an active

republican, who is unemployable between his regular periods
of imprisonment.

They live in a two-up two-down end house in a Catholic
neighbourhood, on the gable wall of which is tarred 'Up the
Republic!', covering the bullet holes where a neighbour, Michael
Fruin, was shot as an informer. The play ends with the daughter,
Monica, seduced, deserted and swindled out of money she holds
for the local slate club, the son shot by the police while 'escaping',
Sar Alice disallowed her sickness benefit and Wallace dead by an
accidental fall from a ladder. Such a catalogue of disasters suggests
an unlikely and inartistic piling-up of gloom and a number of
unresolved sub-plots: the eventual fate of the rebellious Monica
and the position of a typically ambivalent Tomelty character, the
cornet-playing Stewartie, the MacAstockers' lodger who, though
Protestant, and 'raired all your days in Sandy Row', is waiting to
join the Captain Lang Circus band as a cornet player and needs
to learn how to play 'The Soldier's Song'. He is depending upon
his savings from the fund that Monica should be holding to pay
his train fare to Dublin. The character Albert Bonein, who appears
in the *Barnum* plays, is a development of Stewartie and his is the
kind of part that O'Casey used to bring in to heighten the drama
or relieve the tension in a particular scene.

There are obvious parallels with *Juno and the Paycock*, with
Wallace as a less feckless but no less self-deluding Captain Boyle
and Sar Alice as a more harried and less resilient Juno. Seamus
and Monica could be tougher and certainly better written
equivalents for Johnny and Mary Boyle. Some of Wallace's arias
are hilarious, showing in their mixture of imperfectly understood
grand ideas and optimistic fantasies a true grasp of comic writing:

> God! Is it any wonder the nerves are shaking the life out of me?
> Look at my hand – trembling like an aspen leaf. I'm useless. I
> can hardly climb the height of a broomstick. Every time I sit
> down to do a wee bit of thinking my oul' heart is stirred into
> violence again. If it's not my wife's raspy tongue it's the crackling

of bullets or armoured cars jingling the very bed below me. What a bloody environment for a man of imagination.

Coming early in Act I, it establishes Wallace's character in its laziness and pretentiousness and also signals, in a nice piece of dramatic irony, his inevitable fate. In the Abbey production that also featured such later names as Cyril Cusack as Seamus and Siobhan McKenna (using the Irish form of her name, Siobhán Nic Cionnaith) as Monica, McCormick played him as a mixture of Boyle and an unmalevolent Joxer and with such lines as: 'Not that there was a hell of a lot of evil in hitting a peeler', the Abbey audiences could be forgiven for thinking the play comic. It was Siobhan McKenna's first Abbey role and having laddered her stocking on the way to the audition, she was convinced that it would ruin her chances of getting the part. Things were different then.

In many ways it is structurally superior to the O'Casey original that consists of a melodrama interspersed with farce with little interconnection. Joxer and Boyle seem scarcely to belong to the same planet as the rest of the characters. *The End House* is much darker than *Juno and the Paycock* in spite of the looming presence of the Civil War in the latter. Wallace's fear of bullets and armoured cars is real. 'Bates's Harriers', as the Royal Ulster Constabulary (RUC) and the Ulster Special Constabulary (USC) were called, were notably partial, disinclined to tackle Unionist supporters and giving their total attention to the nationalist population. As Wallace observes: 'We all have spirit, but ye get it knocked out of you in this city. I was as bold as ever they made me till the Orangemen kicked my ribs in. "Curse the Pope," says they, and I did curse him.' The prevailing situation is succinctly summed up by the RUC sergeant not long before he shoots Seamus when he tries to run off: 'We'll come when we like, how we like and do what we like.'

The original stimulus for the play was the rage and impotence felt by Northern nationalists with the granting of Bates's special powers and Tomelty's portrayal of the Harriers is highly critical, though he does have one RUC constable with enough kindness to warn the MacAstockers of the possibility of a raid by the heavy squad that evening. His rendering of the characters on what could have been thought to be his own side is equally critical. The character Seamus is stronger and more convincing than his Dublin counterpart, Johnny Boyle, but he covers a kind of moral inertness with doctrinaire republican writ, ready to sacrifice himself to an endless sequence of imprisonment without trial followed by periods of unemployment without dole. The IRA at the time of the play's composition was fairly quiescent, though there were still some diehards active. Local politics, in the person of Joseph Devlin (1871–1934), the northern leader of the old Irish Parliamentary Party who had held West Belfast against de Valera in the Sinn Féin landslide of 1918, were still largely nationalist and constitutional. Seamus's gibe to his father that he'd rather sing, 'God love Johnny Redmond and the Good Old AOH', than fight was true not only of him but of a majority of Catholics at the time. Indeed, many would have sung the hymn more heartily if the words 'Wee Joe' had been substituted for the name of the long-dead Redmond (1856–1918). Though Monica MacAstocker is vain and gullible she has several speeches that give another view to their situation more complex than Seamus's simplistic views can comprehend:

> Yes, I know what you wanted me to be. Captain of the camogie club, collecting money for the Prisoners' Defence Fund. Serving tea and Paris buns at a ceili. Wearing a green frock and showing my thigh as I dance the Fairy Reel. Gaelic respectability.

Perhaps the bitterest description of the misery of the unresolved Irish Question is that uttered by Mrs Fruin, the widow of the man shot as an informer. In O'Casey's play, *The Shadow of a Gunman* (1923), Seumas Shields quotes Ethna Carbery's line: 'Oh! Kathleen Ní Houlihan, your way's a thorny way', as a mantra with little emotional involvement. By contrast in Tomelty's play there is no romantic operatic fervour:

> Will it never cease? What did Ireland want with his life? What did Ireland do for him the three long years he tossed and tumbled on the *Argenta* in Larne Lough and I had to turn out and slave in the mill to feed our weans? What has Ireland done for me? Filled me with hate and tortured me. God curse Ireland. I've cried salt tears and so have my orphans!

The End House was not written quickly but rather matured over several years. Its original stimulus was the cruelty and one-sidedness of the Draconian legislation but it became a play about people, indeed poor people in a community who, having no one else to help them, had to help themselves. In spite of its unresolved sub-plots and its pile-up of death and misery at the end, the play is warm and indeed funny at times. Comparison with O'Casey's play is legitimate, if limited, in use. The MacAstockers are not copies but urban cousins of the Boyles and while *Juno* ends on a note of possibility of hope in the new state, Tomelty offers little for our comfort as the characters spiral deeper into despair, except the confidence that with love people will survive. Considering the final collapse of the UGT, we should not be surprised that the play was not staged in the Group in its prime. It was clearly intended for an Ulster theatre and needed, *pace* the excellence of the Abbey company, the kind of ensemble playing that the UGT for all its shortcomings could provide. The playing of Min Milligan and J.G. Devlin in *The McCooeys* showed what a splendid pair of MacAstockers they could have made. The play's eventual Ulster premiere at the Arts Theatre in 1994 with Mark Mulholland and Barbara Adair as the leads and Roma Tomelty as Mrs Griffith, the extreme republican supporter (called by the author the 'out-and-outer'), was a success.

There was no doubt, however, about the value or the suitability for the Group of *All Souls' Night*, probably Tomelty's finest play, that opened in the Minor Hall in September 1948. He was thirty-seven and well into his power. He took the part of John Quinn, specialising in roles much older than his years. John is the weak, kindly husband of Kathrine, 'a thin, mouthy woman, greedy and seemingly always preoccupied', as the opening stage direction indicates. By dint of hard scraping and general miserliness – 'Hard gathering, my lass, pingeing and mingeing. Waste not, want not' – she has accumulated what is, by her standards, a considerable sum of money, from which she will not use even the interest. Molly, her son Michael's fiancée, who is a clerk in the local post office, urges her in the opening act to use the interest to buy new shoes or a cardigan which, as usual wearing a man's cap with a woollen shawl pinned round her shoulders, she clearly needs.

Her husband and son are forced to make a living with inferior equipment and a dangerously small boat, a fault that could have long ago been rectified if she had made available some of her sterile savings. The action takes place on All Souls' Night, the 2 November, known in the recently lost Irish as *Oiche Fhéile na Marbh* when it was believed that the suffering souls in Purgatory could return to ask for prayers to deliver them out of their temporary torment. The words of the poem with the same title by 'John o' the North' (Harry T. Brown) that is used as epigraph in the printed version of the play are a reminder of this belief:

> For on this night,
> Them that's away
> Could be back again
> Out o' the clay.
>
> They'll come in the dark
> To the warm turf,
> From the coul sod
> And the wet surf.

It is, of all the feasts in the ecclesiastical year, the one obviously dedicated to the 'faithful departed', and it becomes clear that one of the souls to be remembered is Stephen Boyle, the elder son lost at sea.

Tomelty had, with *Red is the Port Light*, already paid his artistic cess (as some of his characters would have put it) to Portaferry and the beautiful and potentially treacherous Strangford Lough, that kind of inner sea, complementing the larger North Channel beyond the long crooked talon of the Ards Peninsula. Now he felt that it should have its dramatic tribute as well. Like every person born in a coastal town, he had a healthy respect for the sea, both for its bounty and its dangers. No sailor himself, he had assimilated sufficient nautical lore from friends and relations to write about it with confidence and accuracy. The inner sea was at its southern end navigable for fairly large vessels and subject to storms as ferocious as in the main. The Quinns are fisherfolk but because of inadequate equipment have to lose many rich catches. The family is dominated by Kathrine who in her absolute, illogical miserliness becomes another of Tomelty's studies in mental imbalance. She was a foundling, and a loveless childhood set a pattern for the rest of her crabbed life. She imposes that aridity on her two sons, one of whom, Stephen, is already dead, having, against every instinct, gone out when 'the ground swell is heavy and the wind is rising in the east' to fetch lobsters for the local landlord: 'I'll have a messenger down for the lobsters at six o'clock, says Sir John.'

In a rare moment of self-awareness and self-revelation she admits that she never laughed as a child, so couldn't as a woman:

> The taste of bitterness was always in my mouth, since I was knee high in the home with the nuns. To be cursed with the want of parents and to be told to be grateful to God for being found in the sheltered hollow of a beech tree. I thought when I married ... But the tree planted crooked will never grow straight ... I thought I would change, that the hardness would leave me.

As the play proceeds – the action continues from early evening until midnight – it becomes clear that John loved someone else and that his brother was hanged for killing a gamekeeper. Both of these facts Kathrine uses against him in their wrangling but in truth she has little respect for him either as a husband or a man. The play's climax, involving the death of the remaining son, is almost inevitable, in that it is only the obliteration of her children that renders her so isolated as to need even the presence – comfort is too strong a word – of her husband. He grants her the absolution of shared responsibility: 'The blame is not all yours. The gap there was between us I helped to widen.' Her penultimate speech gives some ease, a kind of exhausted peace – maybe even catharsis:

> I tried to close it, God knows I did. But the briars of memory would never bind. They seeded from bitterness. A flower must be propped to prosper, a horse haltered. Kindness must be kindled. You planted both in another's womb, you said yourself. We two were only grafted. What flowering can there be on grafted plants?

In the original redaction, John, in grief and despair, kills Kathrine. Stephen says, 'The crying madness overed him when they took your broken body from the sea.' Tomelty's wise friend David Kennedy successfully persuaded him to modify it. As Lena used to say: 'There were more bodies at the end than in *King Lear* ... '

Tomelty, as an artist, always strove to extend the definition of drama. He had shown consummate skill in radio plays, in comedy and in *The End House*, his one overtly political play. Now he was ready to leave naturalism and move into a more theatrical mode, one that reached its culmination in *April in Assagh* (1953). All Souls' Night is celebrated the day after All Hallows, sited deliberately in the Celtic Church close to the pre-Christian *Samhain* that with *Bealtaine* (1 May) marked the axis of the Celtic year. At both these times it was believed the doors to the Otherworld were opened for good or evil and the early Christian Church Christianised the time as one of special concern for the souls in Purgatory. In earlier times priests were allowed to say three Masses on that day, a privilege granted now only at Christmas. Another verse from John o' the North's epigraph poem is applicable here:

And you in the loft
Can breathe a prayer
For the wakin' dead
That's gathered there.

The ghosts of Stephen and Michael and describe in a detached, non-accusatory way, that is all the more effective in its sense of remoteness from earthly concerns, how they died. Stephen appears first as if summoned by the ritual prayers said by his father: 'Eternal rest, O Lord, grant to the soul of my dead son, Stephen, and let perpetual light shine upon him … ' It becomes clear that Stephen was terrified of the sea and dreaded heading out to check the pots for lobsters for Sir John, while his mother insisted that: 'The gentry are good people, good people.' He is joined by the dead Michael, who in his desperate efforts to get enough money for a down payment to buy the *Maid of Trostan*, a better and safer boat on offer at a reasonable price, goes scavenging a ship, wrecked in Kintaugh Bay, a known 'treacherous' part. (One of the tragic ironies of his sacrifice is that Thurston, the bank manager who had refused to lend him the money, is persuaded to change his mind by Molly and intends to do business with him next day).

The dramatic possibilities of a revenant called up by a similar death were almost impossible to resist, especially when Tomelty found an appropriate register for the spectral language that the ghosts used. In the play, the sea's presence is overwhelming and it helped the author generate some heightened, quasi-poetic dialogue that is highly effective dramatically:

STEPHEN: The two of us now.
MICHAEL: Yes. At the Bruin Perch. Close to the warted perch. The blistered weed clipped my fingers, curled its heavy weave about my arms, circled in a net around my neck, pocking its

tartled tails in my eyes, until the swirling tide poured death into
me.

Later, Stephen accuses his mother of being the remote cause
of both their deaths: 'My own last thoughts were against herself.
A spurt of anger spitting after life as it left me,' while Michael
tries to find a cause if not an excuse: 'The whinge of poverty that
drowned her soul, washing out the finer things.'

If one were asked the impossible question beloved of
interviewers as to which single item of an author's work one might
preserve while the rest perished, it would have to be *All Souls'
Night.* It does not show Tomelty's remarkable capacity for comedy
nor his acute ear for urban working-class language. It does,
however, contain many of his moral and psychological
preoccupations. There is the almost pathological absorption in
madness or lesser mental imbalance, specified by John Quinn
when he cries out at the beginning of Act III: 'Sometimes I think
there's a kind of madness in this house.' The character of Kathrine
with her obsessive need to scrimp and save amounts to a case
history and she is full sister to Frankie Price's unhappy aunt in
The Apprentice.

Tomelty would have been the first to admit that apart from her
own distorted psyche, one reason for Kathrine's hoarding of money
to no obvious purpose was the ingrained poverty that afflicted
the North during his formative years. His own childhood, as the
eldest of seven children, had been Spartan and a kind of watchful
frugality returned for a time after his accident. When John and
Molly discuss her intended marriage to Michael he is anxious that
she be more loving and maternal than Kathrine:

> You wouldn't push them away from you, like they do about these
> doors? They're like the swans you'd see in the Glendry bog,
> Molly. They chase their young from them when the first signs
> of whiteness are on them. That's what they do with their weans
> here. When the down comes on their cheeks, off with the boys
> to sea and the girls to service.

Tomelty had been 'chased' himself and some residual bitterness remained. Because of the size of the local community in the play there is little or no space or need for rival tribal camps. Though there is no recorded evidence of Tomelty himself being expelled from the shipyard during times of sectarian tension, it was part of the family history that his father, Rollickin' James, had been driven out from where he had previously worked on the *Titanic* because he was a Catholic. He had managed to hitchhike to Downpatrick and eventually found a boat to take him across the lough to his home.

It is also, like many great dramas, a risk-taking venture; the inclusion of elements of the supernatural in an otherwise naturalistic work required nerve, but with the excellence of the acting of Maurice O'Callaghan as Michael and James Young, later known as a comedian, as Stephen, it worked triumphantly – and still does. The part of Kathrine was taken by Elizabeth Begley, one of the Group's strongest leads and as for Tomelty's performance as the gentle, put-upon, finally forgiving John Quinn, the part could literally have been written for him. This is perhaps best realised in the tender little cameo scene in Act II in which Molly begins to teach him 'letters and numbers':

> And that's a nought. Round like a sail ring or the eye of a herrin'. And that's a five shaped like a cup hook in the dresser and a six like what a worm would ooze on the beach. As you say, Molly, it would be no time before I could write and read.

The lesson leads to a sad note of triumph near the end of the play when he is just able to read the amount of money that Kathrine has saved through her family's forced privation, repeating: 'A five, shaped like a cup hook that you'd see in a dresser, and noughts like the round eyes of a herring.'

Finally, the play complements *Red is the Port Light* as a word portrait of the land of lost content, the environment that shaped Tomelty, however urbanised he became or how much he loved

Carnlough. He listed placenames and regional vocabulary as a kind of mantra, aware of what in Irish is called *dinnseanchas,* the numinous quality of local habitation and name. As we hear the words Rock Angus, Corrig Reef, Paddy Lug, Jackdaw Island, Kearney Point, Gunn's Isle, Isle o' Valley, the Gowlings, Swan Rock, the long Sheelahs, Tara Bay, Kintaugh Bay, the Glendry Bog, Cloughey and Bruin Perch, names significant to the characters, the effect is not one of alienation but of invitation to share this remarkable topography. It is a piece of literary prestidigitation as cheeky and successful as the introduction of the ghosts of Stephen and Michael. Though Tomelty never actually sailed in a smack or trawler, he collected the local names for fish, boats and seaweed, and knew the location of all the reefs and currents in the lough. In his many trips abroad for stage work and filming, he preferred, when possible, to travel by steamer rather than plane. In those years there were regular sailings to Glasgow, Ardrossan, Stranraer, Heysham and Liverpool. As for the shore-based sailor, he made a practice of staying up on deck until he lost sight of Ireland, in the last case the Copeland Islands off Donaghadee.

12
The Passing Day

IN 1951, AFTER SIX YEARS OF austerity under the Labour government of Clement Attlee (1883–1967) essentially in its last months, it was decided to reward the British public with the Festival of Britain. It was sold partly as a centenary of the great Victorian exhibition of 1851 initiated by Victoria's consort Prince Albert to demonstrate Britain's supremacy in industry. The six post-war years had been tough, with rationing and shortages worse even than during the war. Now there were signs that the grimmer days were passing and, besides, the ailing administration could be doing with some positive publicity. The task was given to Attlee's great rival Herbert Morrison (1888–1965), the Leader of the House of Commons. Each sizable town in the United Kingdom was expected to take part and London itself built the Festival Hall, the first cultural structure on the South Bank since the days of Shakespeare's Globe. J.B. Priestley wrote a mildly satirical novel called *Festival at Farbridge* and Noel Coward summed up the general ambivalence with a revue song called 'Don't Make Fun of the Fair', that contained the lines:

Don't make fun of the festival.
Don't make fun of the fair.
We downtrodden British must learn to be skittish
And give an impression of devil-may-care ...

Northern Ireland was required to contribute and there was no ambivalence on the part of the government. There was a huge Farm and Factory exhibition at Castlereagh where the 'new' artistic concept of the mobile was first unveiled to Ulster eyes. A vocal arts lobby demanded a greater aesthetic element in the festivities and succeeded in obtaining the finance for a season of plays at the Grand Opera House and an elegant volume about all aspects of local artistic life to be called *The Arts in Ulster*, edited by Sam Hanna Bell. The latter was an early summary of remarkably rich cultural activity, of the sort that the Stormont government, perhaps rightly, regarded as subversive. The financial conduit was CEMA. Its successor, the Arts Council of Northern Ireland, removed the nominal dichotomy. It had the positive effect of establishing Bell, then forty-two, as a significant member of the aesthetic establishment of Northern Ireland.

One useful feature of *The Arts in Ulster* was a series of full- or half-page photographs of writers, including Joseph Campbell (1879–1944), William Carleton (1794–1860), Stephen Gilbert (1912–2010), Forrest Reid (1875–1947), W.R. Rodgers (1909–69), St John Ervine (1883-1971) – and Tomelty. In fact Gilbert was a late insertion, replacing Michael McLaverty (1904–92) who did not wish to be associated with so British an event. As he wrote to Bell the previous September: 'You don't expect an Irish nationalist like myself to subscribe, implicitly or explicitly, to Festival activities. I couldn't do so until our broken country is healed.' He spoke for a majority of his fellows.

In the volume's coverage of literature and drama by, respectively, John Boyd (1912–2002) and David Kennedy, it was significant that Tomelty's name occurred in both chapters. By then he and the main editor had each one novel to his credit,

Bell's Hardyean *December Bride*, just published that year and one of the finest Irish novels ever published, while Tomelty's *Red is the Port Light* (1948) was barely three years old, not far behind it in literary quality and certainly as imaginative and moving as Bell's, both coincidentally set against a background of the treacherously beautiful Strangford Lough in County Down. Boyd was a close friend of both men but he was an austere critic with an academic background. He duly praised their excellence but found it necessary to point out what he considered to be some flaws in structure.

David Kennedy, though like Michael McLaverty a science graduate, had made himself an authority on Irish drama, with especial reference to the Ulster Literary Theatre (ULT), mentioned earlier, which was founded by Bulmer Hobson (1883–1969) and David Parkhill in 1902. *Enter Robbie John*, his documentary radio programme commissioned and produced by Sam Hanna Bell in November 1954, told the story of that theatrical movement that began, according to Hobson, on the GNR train back to Belfast. They had gone to visit the giants of the Irish Literary Theatre, Lady Gregory, Dudley Digges (1879–1947), Maud Gonne and the great posturing mage himself and had been received warmly by all the company (not yet the Abbey actors) except Yeats (1865–1939). As their train headed for north Dublin, Hobson broke the silence by striking the armrest and crying: 'Damn Yeats! We'll write our own plays.' They found in Sam Waddell (1878–1967), brother of the medieval scholar Helen Waddell (1889–1965), who also wrote for the ULT, the defining playwright of the movement. He, writing as Rutherford Mayne, produced *The Turn of the Road* (1906) in which the gifted Robbie John has to choose between life as a musician and life on an Ulster farm and *The Drone* (1908), the first and most famous example of that strange literary form, the Ulster play.

Other dramatists associated with the ULT such as Lynn Doyle – originally the jokey title 'Lynn C. Doyle' – the pseudonym of

Leslie A. Montgomery (1873–1961), and especially George Shiels (1886–1949), continued to supply the Abbey with the bitter comedies that helped it survive. One writer, Charles Kerr, a schoolmaster, followed the practice, considered by some necessary, of using a pseudonym. Waddell had become Rutherford Mayne and Montgomery Lynn Doyle. Harry C. Morrow (1866–1938) the author of the famous ULT satirical squib, *Thompson in Tír na nÓg* (1912) had hidden under the name Gerald MacNamara and now Kerr used the form C.K. Ayre. It was he who placed Tomelty's first piece of writing with the BBC and netted him a fee of 20 guineas – 'a fortune', as Tomelty afterwards described it. Indeed it had the buying power of £1,000 in today's currency. It was produced by Larry Morrow, who had been a journalist in Dublin and London and to whom *Red is the Port Light*, Tomelty's first novel, was dedicated. This was a version of *The Beauty Competition* that he had written for the St Peter's Players. It would afterwards go through several reincarnations, first as *Barnum Was Right* and later as the very successful *Mugs and Money* (1953).

Kennedy's survey followed his brief, precisely telling the story of 'The Drama in Ulster' from the earliest times up until the year of the festival. He sketched in the founding and development of the ULT's chief successor, the Ulster Group Theatre discussed earlier, naming as the Group's chief sources of plays the trio: St John Ervine, George Shiels and Joseph Tomelty. It is not entirely a matter of coincidence that one of the Shiels plays he mentions is *The Passing Day* (1936), which he describes as 'a realistic study, etched in acid, of an Ulster businessman'. He was almost certainly aware that Tyrone Guthrie (1900–71) had chosen it as one of a trio of 'local' plays that were to represent Ulster's contribution to the festival. The others were *Danger, Men Working!* by John D. Stewart, a play of contemporary Ulster life, and *The Sham Prince*, a not too scurrilous Restoration comedy by Charles Shadwell (?1675–1726). For the last of these, Jack Loudan, the Armagh playwright, transposed the setting to Belfast and gave James Young the opportunity to prove that he was one of the finest and most adaptable of the UGT's actors in his role as Trip, the resourceful valet, a fact that tended to be forgotten when he broadened his comedy into extremely funny but limited caricature. Tomelty himself had a peach of a part as the affected dandy Sir Bullet Airy and Min Milligan played, as though born for Restoration roles, Mrs Twist, a devious lacemaker.

Kennedy declared that Tomelty was the most interesting of the younger dramatists and praised *Right Again, Barnum,* 'high on the list of Group successes' from 'a master of the Belfast idiom'. He also mentioned *The End House,* 'a realistic play about Belfast's back streets' that 'had its first production at the Abbey Theatre in 1944'. Interestingly, he could sense Tomelty's desire to move 'away from the confining bonds of realism which may prove to be his most valuable contribution to the theatre', mentioning how the 'vein of poetic fantasy' was 'hinted at in an early play, *Idolatry at Innishargie* and had fuller expression in his latest play, *All Souls' Night*':

> With a masterly sense of the evocative power of words Tomelty builds up, drop by drop, as it were, the surge of the sea on the rocky coast of his native Ards and matches its waves with the emotional surge in the hearts of these fisherfolk.

Considering the constraints of space and the wariness that was a requirement for any writer in an establishment-promoted publication in those years, the essay was an astute and deft summary of the forty-year-old's achievement.

Kennedy was also asked to contribute to the twentieth and final number of *Rann,* the 'Ulster Quarterly: Poetry and Comment' (June 1953), edited by Barbara Edwards and Roy McFadden, another essay on contemporary drama with the specific title, 'The Theatre in Ulster: 1944–1953'. By the time the essay was written the success of the festival play *The Passing*

Day in London had brought the Ulster theatre to the notice of West End playgoers and had incidentally launched Tomelty on a career as a film actor:

> This play had a great success in London when produced there by Tyrone Guthrie for the Festival of Britain in 1951. The London production was especially notable for Joseph Tomelty's performance in the leading role of John Fibbs ... [His] *Right Again, Barnum* was high on the list of the Group's popular successes. His *Idolatry at Innishargie* and *Poor Errand* were interesting though not successful. More effective were *The End House* and *All Souls' Night*, which had Abbey as well as Group Theatre productions. Since Tomelty's London success in *The Passing Day*, he has been lost, at least temporarily to Belfast. His influence as a writer and an actor of outstanding talent played a considerable part in making the Group Theatre a truly Ulster theatre during the years he worked there.

John Boyd wrote about Ulster novels as he had done in the festschrift. As before his coverage was inevitably limited to thumbnail sketches in the space of the equivalent of two A4 pages. Slightly quixotically he decided to move backwards, beginning with the most recently published Ulster novel and ending with the works of William Carleton. By chance, *The Apprentice*, Tomelty's second novel, was published that same year and Boyd led with it, opining that: 'Tomelty keeps within the range of his experience and he is thoroughly familiar with the milieu of this novel', which is a slightly mandarin way of saying that in *The Apprentice*, uniquely among working-class novels, the actual nature of the work is given in comprehensive and accurate detail. Even after a second reading he finds the wilder and more atmospheric *Red is the Port Light* 'perhaps a less successful novel'. He does praise Tomelty's 'qualities of easy narration and swift economical dialogue':

> ... it is the dialogue of a dramatist. And in fact Tomelty has written at least one remarkable poetic play in *All Souls' Night*

and a serious realistic play in *The End House*. Besides being a writer he is an outstanding actor of great versatility.

It was this versatility that caused Guthrie to choose him to play the lead in the first of the Festival plays. The choice of Guthrie as director was unusually imaginative by the members of the CEMA Festival committee. There was no doubt about his Ulster credentials: his mother was a granddaughter of Tyrone Power, the great Irish actor-manager (1795–1841), and her home at Annaghmakerrig, County Monaghan, was to play a major part in Guthrie's life and become his aesthetic legacy to Ireland. His was the first voice heard on 15 September 1924 when '2BE, the Belfast Station of the British Broadcasting Corporation' began broadcasting from 31 Linenhall Street. He would have loved to have become an actor but his height of 6'6" precluded him from most stage parts. By 1951 he had a worldwide reputation as an *enfant terrible* with at times a wild enthusiasm for the theatre. His time at the Old Vic – 1933 to 1946 with occasional gaps – laid the basis for Britain's National Theatre and moulded the careers of Charles Laughton (1899–1962), Flora Robson (1902–84), Ralph Richardson (1902–1983), Peggy Ashcroft (1907–91), Laurence Olivier (1907–89) and Alec Guinness (1914–2000). His production of *Hamlet* in 1937 in which Guinness, playing the lead, smoked many cigarettes lit with his own lighter, and moved through an Elsinore court where all wore evening dress, caused a sensation, as did his production in 1962 of Ben Jonson's *The Alchemist* in which whores in short nightdresses listened to transistor radios.

The Passing Day gave no scope for his trademark crowd choreography, being literally a set piece, but he managed the need for constantly shifting locales by using a triptych set with spotlighting to indicate change while behind was the bed in which Fibbs lay and in which he would die. Guthrie had seen the Group in action and picked out Tomelty as the man to play the protagonist – he could not by any means be called a hero. The author George Shiels had been born near Ballymoney, County Antrim, had emigrated to Canada and been grievously injured while working on the Canadian Pacific Railway. He was confined to a wheelchair for the rest of his life. He died just two years before the choice by Guthrie of what many regarded as his best play. He had been writing plays since his return to his homeland and had been one of the early ULT dramatists. The bitter nature of his comedies, staged mainly by the Abbey management, and showing, at best, a cynical view of his fellow Ulstermen, was attributed, perhaps simplistically, to his physical condition. Yet even his 'good' characters tend to be glib and as full of chicanery as his villains.

On page 5 of a 1976 letter to his daughter Roma when she was at the University of York, Tomelty reminded her that Shiels had a very limited experience of actual theatre. It is believed that because of his disability the only one of his plays that he had seen performed on stage was an Abbey production of *Professor Tim* (1925) in Belfast that he watched from the wings. Noting that 'Shiels was tied to a wheelchair', Tomelty averred that it:

> ... denied him the freedom one needs in any theatre, if one wants to write. I recall him telling me, 'How lucky you are to be working in a theatre.' When we broadcast *Passing Day* I played Looney [the solicitor]. He didn't think there was so much in the part ... it makes me think had he been able to visit theatres his work might not have been so esoterical. He would have learned the dos and don'ts.

The letter ends with a threnody for the demise of his typewriter: ' ... no shame for it. Anything I have written, it did me well'. (This was the same typewriter on which, as children, having climbed on their father's knee, Roma and Frances were allowed to pick out their names before being shooed into silence to 'let Daddy get on with his work'). A postscript reminds Roma about the Pecksniffian attitudes of the broadcasting godfathers in the matter of language:

> At one time we were not allowed to say 'God' in the Belfast
> BBC. It had to be 'my Golly' and 'I don't give a dang' for 'I
> don't give a damn'.

The clarity and coherence of thought in the mid-'70s letter
show just how close to normality Tomelty had become after the
trauma of the brain injury sustained in April 1955 that effectively
ended his career as a writer.

The broadcast production referred to in the letter may be that
of *His Last Day in Business*, a radio play commissioned by BBC
Northern Ireland, from which the stage play was generated, though
in its later format it remained extremely suitable for radio
broadcasting. As the original title indicates, it describes the events
of the day on which a small-town wholesale and retail merchant
eventually succumbs to a terminal stroke. The play eschews the
usual three-act format, for action inevitably involves flashbacks,
including the significant one that takes Fibbs back to his childhood
and shows how he was frustrated in his desire to emigrate to
America by a father even more cheese-paring than he, and a
mother patently out of love with her husband and anxious for his
death:

> Your da's in bad health, a wake heart. The Doctor says he might
> go out like a match ... then we'll be rid of him.

Though a similar hope is never expressed verbally by Fibbs's
charmless grasping wife, it is made clear by the dialogue that it is
her dearest wish. Christopher Fitz-Simon in his book, *The Irish
Theatre* (1983), cannot help noting that though the play is funny,
' ... there is not one character whose actions are motivated by
other than self-interest'. Still, he found the play Molieresque and
even a modern morality, though thought it unlikely that such ideas
ever occurred to Shiels. And yet some dramaturgical instinct
prompted Shiels, however unwittingly, to write an Ulster
Everyman. The parallels are striking: in the fifteenth-century play
Death comes for Everyman and he invites his terrestrial

acquaintances, personified as Kindred, Knowledge, Beauty, Worldly Goods, Strength, Good Deeds and others to accompany him. Only Good Deeds stays with him and after a salutary and strengthening visit to Confession he makes his way fearlessly to wherever Death will take him.

In *The Passing Day*, destiny comes in the form of a stroke and the play opens in the waiting room of a hospital behind which, in Guthrie's production, one could see Tomelty unconscious in the bed. (The artist Markey Robinson, short of digs in London, slept on this bed at night in the theatre). The picture of him lying there, though hardly a startling idea, caught the fancy of the British newspapers. They printed it as if it were somehow revolutionary – another Guthrie ploy. The next four scenes rehearse what the original radio script suggests, his last day of business. As Fitz-Simon suggests, the visits of a string of clients could become morality archetypes. The parallels are not exact but the doctor might easily stand for Health, Daw, his solicitor, Worldy Wiseman, his rapacious wife and nephew very unloving Kindred, a prying tax inspector, Nemesis, and even a gravedigger. The production in its remorseless exposure of the venal nature of its characters took on some of the strength of the Dutch original and the character of Fibbs was a part for Tomelty 'to tear a cat in', as Bottom wanted to in *A Midsummer Night's Dream*. He showed a very muddy Everyman in his parsimony, double-dealing, cowardice, lying and unrelenting greed, and yet there was not a member of the audience who did not feel sympathy for him or who did not feel a surge of delight when both his unloving wife and peculating nephew are done out of their legacy.

The new will that would have made them the chief beneficiaries could not be signed because of Fibbs's death and all his considerable wealth goes to the only person who showed him any real affection, his sister Rachel who lives in Clydebank. It was truly an Everyman part and there was no one better equipped than Tomelty to show the insecurity, the concomitant fear that possesses every miser and the little loveless child under all the cheating, lying and bullying. Though it may not have been clear beyond the sixth row of the stalls, he had a great face, able to show the kaleidoscope of emotions that passed across it in the course of a few minutes, with a kind of bewilderment at his barely perceived and only dimly understood contradictions of character. The voice had the same capacity for change: cruel, sneaky, crafty – and intermittently generous – as if to its owner's surprise and slipping easily from bluster to bleat. His appearance, described in *Quinlan's Illustrated Directory of Film Character Actors* (1995), as 'thick-set ... with a bush of silver hair' gave a sense of great physical strength. Yet in an instant he could seem to crumple into weakness, his sinews no longer able to bear him stiffly up.

For the purposes of the festival dramas, Guthrie set up a new company known as the Northern Ireland Festival Players. Tomelty was an obvious choice for Fibbs but there were complications. When Harold Goldblatt heard of the possibility of the formation of a new Ulster company he reverted to a not uncharacteristic authoritarian stance. The UGT had many virtues, good acting and ensemble playing and a convincing delivery of Ulster plays, but interpersonal relations between the different strands that made up the woven fabric were not good. Goldblatt and R.H. McCandless, both fine actors, assumed an authority for which there was no obvious entitlement. Even when Tomelty was business manager and undertook every other task imposed on him, he was not regarded as of equal status. His plays, which had contributed greatly to the success of the UGT venture, had to be submitted to the self-appointed tribunal. He was regularly kept waiting for weeks for a decision. He was often urged to broaden the comedy: 'Fall on your arse!', as one of them crudely advised.

When word of the casting of *The Passing Day* came to Goldblatt's ears, he uttered an ultimatum: 'If you go with Guthrie don't come back. You'll never work in this town again!' It was something of a blow to the forty-year-old with two children aged six and four, and no regular income. Sam Hanna Bell describes in the profile mentioned above how he found him one night sitting as usual in the Group's little box office in Bedford Street, 'swithering over the alternatives facing him'. Time was pressing and finally he came to a decision: 'I said to myself I'll go to London and if Ivor Brown, the critic, says: "Tomelty shouldn't be on the stage at all," well, I'll get off it for good.' Bell's conclusion to the story was succinct: 'Ivor Brown didn't say that; in fact he said quite the reverse.' Brown (1891–1974) was the magisterial drama critic of the *Observer*, the other posh Sunday with the *Sunday Times*, which had Harold Hobson (1904–92) as drama critic. Their reviews had a significant effect on the commercial viability of any West End play and Brown approved strongly of *The Passing Day* and its lead.

Though the UGT had expressed its disapproval of Group actors joining Guthrie's Festival Company, many of the ones astutely chosen had played in the theatre. These were almost entirely Ulster actors and as such most appropriate for *The Passing Day*; they included J.G. Devlin (1907–1991), even then famous as Granda McCooey in the long-running soap written by Tomelty, who played the tax inspector, Patrick McAlinney (1913–90) as the beset grocer Looney, James Young as a commercial traveller and Patrick Magee (1924–82) as the doctor. These all found stage, film and television careers afterwards in Britain, Magee noted for his interpretation of the plays of Friel and Beckett. *The Passing Day* opened on Monday, 7 May 1951 in the Grand Opera House and ran for a week. The *Belfast News Letter*'s reporter said that Tomelty, 'who has long since won his place in Ulster theatre gave a performance that will rank in the greatest in his distinguished career'. The Group, in a weak attempt at competition, put on an old reliable well-made three-acter by one of their house authors, St John Ervine, *Friends and Relations* (1941), that had its first

production at the Abbey ten years previously and also dealt with
the effects of a last will and testament upon a family, though in
this one the family was urban and middle-class. *Danger, Men
Working!* followed on Monday, 14 May and *The Sham Prince*, a
play nearer to Guthrie's heart and theatrical taste, ran from 28
May for a fortnight, ending a triumphant theatrical month on
Saturday, 3 June.

Tomelty enjoyed working with Guthrie – they soon became
'Joe' and 'Tony' – and would often meet in Dublin for coffee and
chat. Since both men had to be 'careful' with money, Guthrie
always tossed a coin to see who would pay. One aspect of Guthrie's
direction throws more light on UGT practice than on that of the
Festival players. Shiels's lines had been known DLP ('dead letter
perfect'), an insistence that became nightmarish for Tomelty who,
with his flair for invention, often gave extempore paraphrases on
stage of the author's script (including his own). He managed to
learn the lines as written; he had always considered earlier
divagations from script in other plays as on-the-spot improvements.
Several fellow members of the UGT ensemble were also chosen
to be part of the company. They included John McBride, James
Young and Tomelty's mother-in-law, Min Milligan, all of whom
figured regularly in *The McCooeys*. Min greatly impressed
Guthrie by offering to take her teeth out for the part of the ghost
of Fibbs's mother in the Dickensian flashback scene of his younger
life, that like the Fezziwig episode in *A Christmas Carol* goes some
way to excuse the meanness of his character. When Min was asked
if she had an agent she replied: 'Of course. Crotty & Aiken' – her
estate agents. An example of *in* the theatre but not *of* it!

The play, as was intended, transferred to London and played
at the New Ambassador's Theatre. The film *Odd Man Out*, now
four years old, had become a kind of cult movie, in the top ten list
of many critics. Carol Reed was at the height of his career, having
made *The Fallen Idol* and *The Third Man*. His films were studied
by his fellow professionals and the word that 'Gin' Jimmy was

appearing in the West End brought to the theatre, among other cineastes, David Lean (1908–91), whose career was also on the rise. He had shown his skill in sophisticated comedy with *Blithe Spirit* (1945), in romance with the flawless *Brief Encounter* (1945) and two brilliant versions of Dickens, *Great Expectations* and *Oliver Twist*. Now he was beginning to film *The Sound Barrier*, a fictionalised account of aircraft with speeds greater than that of sound and he decided that Tomelty was ideal for the part of Will Sparks, the clever tousled backroom boy with his magic slide rule. Another significant showbiz person also saw the play and made an appointment to see the new actor. This was Frederick Joachim, a theatrical agent whose list of clients included Thora Hird, Dirk Bogarde and Peter Illing (1899–1966). Maxine, Illing's wife, told Lena Tomelty that while Joachim was on friendly terms with all his clients, he *loved* Tomelty and continued to find him work after his accident.

Tomelty had arrived as an accredited and reliable character actor, who between 1946 and 1964 would make thirty films. Quinlan's summary: 'He played whimsical roles ... mostly as helpful old codgers in shabby waistcoats and rolled-up sleeves' is a reasonable generalisation but not the whole picture. Lean used him again in *Hobson's Choice* (1954), a classic realisation of the famous comedy by Harold Brighouse (1882–1958), written for the Gaiety Theatre in Manchester in 1916. It was one of a series of plays written for Annie Horniman's (1860–1937) Manchester School of Theatre, to which she turned after leaving the Abbey, disappointed in Yeats, aesthetically, politically and sexually. The story concerns Harold Hobson, a bullying drunken cobbler, whose 'plain' but indispensable daughter Maggie outsmarts him by marrying his downtrodden, clever craftsman, Willie Mossop. It has been revived many times since, deservedly so and Lean's film has never been bettered. Charles Laughton played Hobson, John Mills (1908–2005), Willie and Brenda de Banzie (1901–81), Maggie. Tomelty played Jim Heeler, one of

Hobson's toadies. He was required to grow a beard for the part. The result gave him a strange pied appearance and, as mentioned previously, Roma and Frances were startled and slightly dismayed to find that when their father came home on a few days' break from shooting, his hair was white, his sideburns black and his beard ginger.

13
The Apprentice

TOMELTY'S SECOND NOVEL, *THE Apprentice*, appeared in 1953, published, like the first, by Jonathan Cape. Its subtitle, 'The Story of a Nonentity', prepares us for a tale of inadequacy, inevitable cruelty and a painful prolonged rite of passage. There is nothing ambivalent about that description, unlike the self-conscious *Diary of a Nobody* (1892) by George (1847–1912) and Weedon (1852–1919) Grossmith, in which the eponymous Charles Pooter scarcely believes the title and does not really live up to it. Francis Price, when we first meet him at age fourteen, is undersized, enuretic, acrophobic, stammering, orphaned and inescapably self-pitying and inert. His guardian, a maiden aunt, treats him abominably and seems to centre the deep unhappiness of her own life on him as scapegoat. She is a monster of pious cruelty and the bored and insensitive priest brought in to discipline the mildly wayward nephew takes her side without question as he attempts to crush the wrongdoer. In the interview with his friend John Boyd, referred to in the first chapter, Tomelty says that one of the stimuli for writing the book was the German novel *Kleiner Mann, Was Nun?* (1932) by Hans Fallada (1893–1947). It describes the straits that a young couple are driven to with a baby and no work in the last days of the Weimar republic. The main link is poverty and the absolute wretchedness of the sensitive in a world of cruel competition but at least the protagonist Pinneberg and his 'lambkin' Emma find some ease in their mutual love. Frankie the apprentice has a much longer journey to travel before he finds rest.

The novel has a triple aspect; its elements of autobiography are valuable since the geniality and ebullience that characterised the adult Tomelty often hid a not entirely happy childhood. The detail of the stammering of his chief character was part of his own childhood. The schoolmaster in the novel who uses the dismissive term 'bug-blinder' for Frankie's intended avocation and unnecessarily draws attention to his stature as 'two hands higher than a duck', suggesting that he might sue the Corporation 'for bumping your bottom on the pavement', may also have drawn from real life. The reader cannot help relishing the fact that the teacher's laugh is cut short when he has to close 'his mouth suddenly as his false teeth dropped'. Gibes like: 'Be sure to put the paint right side out' were common and often meant lightly but the teacher made them hurt. The mixture of impatience and rough kindness shown by the painters on the job rings absolutely true and the gradual increase in competence at the work – in Frankie's case very gradual – is nicely handled. Frankie's physical inadequacy is unsentimentally underscored with the introduction of an apprentice replacement, who 'can skip up and down ladders and over that plank like a bloody monkey'.

The second aspect of the book is its sense of place in city and country. In its oblique way it delineates sights, sounds and smells of the Belfast of the 1930s in its last feverish radiance of Linenopolis, with its factory horns and 'knockers-up' who were paid to rattle doors before six o'clock, as effectively as the paintings of L.S. Lowry (1887–1976) do for the Ancoats of the same period. In contrast to *Red is the Port Light*, the endemic sectarianism of '30s Belfast (and later) as shown in *The Apprentice* is overt and all the more noisome. In Portaferry the population is relatively small and there is no space for ghettoes. Both sides of the house, to use the dire Ulsterism, need each other's help to survive. Working-class Belfast with its virtually hermetically sealed tribal areas had been notorious for regularly recurring sectional violence from the 1840s while two separate peoples lived lives of mutual suspicion glorifying their own culture, if that word may be used. The location of the house of freethinking Molly, the woman who becomes Frankie's final salvation, is in Tomb Street, lying between the commercial quarter of the city and the docks – an area truly 'mixed'. It was a deliberate, maybe even symbolic, choice by Tomelty. Perhaps it is not too fanciful to see a resigned hopelessness in the choice of name for even though it is an actual street, once the location of the mail sorting office, there is a sense that Belfast troubles may never be settled on this side of the grave.

Tomelty had lived in Belfast since he was a teenager, in digs in Dover Street that ran from the bottom of the Falls at Divis Street to Peter's Hill at the foot of the Shankill, and elsewhere in the district. He was literally in the centre of the violence and the mental searing of the time found its exorcism in *The End House*. The precise dating of *The Apprentice* is not given but strands of internal evidence suggest a slightly earlier period. Simon Clarke, one of Frankie's few friends, 'would never speak of the King, but always of Geordie the Fifth', who died in 1936. There is no hint of current urban violence but it is felt along the nerve-ends and acts as an implicit backdrop to the urban scene. The Hitler war with its terrible air raids does not seem to have been experienced by any of the characters and the economic conditions as to wages and living conditions adumbrated would fit the mid-1930s. The interlude when Frankie pays for a night in a dosshouse, 'lodgings for men', has an authentic latter-day Dickensian atmosphere.

In the end, of course, it must be judged as a novel, a piece of extended prose, attempting to delineate real life, whose main purpose is to entertain. If this definition is accepted, *The Apprentice* fits it very well. There are sentimental passages: the character of Molly, Frankie's eventual saviour and sexual partner, has an element of male fantasy about it but it provides a fitting fictive resolution. His aunt, who may owe a little to Tomelty's own great-aunt who was his first Belfast landlady, at times seems one-dimensional in her relentless cruelty but her patriotic exaltation and obsessive dedication to the cause for which her fiancé died is so well expressed that the author must clearly have met with and disapproved of such fanaticism. She has been a strong IRA supporter and did time in jail for attempting to smuggle messages to Republican prisoners in Crumlin Road jail. Her normal emotional life finished when her fiancé was shot during the Belfast pogrom of the early 1920s and his framed photograph is the centre of a little domestic shrine emblazoned with the words: 'He died for Ireland.'

This obsession is aggravated by the shame that her dead brother, Frankie's father, had enlisted in the British army. With a characteristic twinge of the grotesque Tomelty has endowed him with a wooden arm on which he tests the sharpness of his penknife, 'shaving off little ribbons. When he put the knife away he would take a little bottle of stain from the mantelpiece and stain the new whiteness of the arm'. It is the only clear memory that Frankie retains of his dead father. His mother, who died when he was three, has left no trace. She is described by Simon Clarke, a mate of his father and one of the boy's few sources of care, as 'a wee angel of a woman with just the smallest cast in her eye; and yet do you know, far from it having an unsightly effect, I must say it made her face more attractive'.

In spite of having little natural competence in his avocation, and beset by his acrophobia, Frankie survives to become a recognised tradesman and in the usual way of that world is immediately dismissed. This brings about a bloody confrontation with his aunt and his final sloughing of her from his life. He has developed for the nonce sufficient coherence of speech to dismiss the embarrassed priest sent by her to win him back to 'respectability'. He realises that opportunities for work are limited:

> He knew Turnbull was right. The shipyard usually employed only Protestants but when they were busy they took on Catholics.

An older man, Sylvester Haig, once his foreman and now married to a niece of his friend Simon Clarke, offers him an acceptable job as a storesman but with a sudden burst of uncharacteristic pride Frankie considers it a slight and a sign that no one accepts his status as tradesman. Yet he has made himself a competent glazier and it is this skill that brings him under the care of the woman nearly twice his age, with a child that she refers to as her 'little souvenir', who eventually makes a man of him. Her kindness and enthusiasm – and total lack of the cancerous sectarianism that blights the Belfast of the 1930s – restores him to a kind of peace, provides him with a gait of going.

The contrast with the aunt is plangent; her miserliness, her cruelty, her wretched lack of kindness make her almost too much of a monster. She stands a type of those who spread unease and misery as thickly laid on as Molly's cosy kindness. Significantly her forename is never mentioned and the relentlessness of her campaign against her nephew becomes almost a parody of right living. Her greed and slovenliness – and general relish of unhappiness – are only partly explicable by grief at the loss of her 'martyred' fiancé. Her attitude to Frankie and the general unending harshness of her behaviour suggest that she is close to mental imbalance, a subject that continued to fascinate the author in all its manifestations. Hers is the kind of joyless *unco guidness* that one associates more with extreme evangelism than the intended joyfulness of Catholicism.

The bitter parody of the 1914 Wenrich & Mahoney ragtime

song, 'When You Wore a Tulip' sung by Toby Mackin, one of the painters, harks back to the Great War:

> When I wore the khaki, the dark coloured khaki,
> You wore your civvy clothes.
> I fought and bled at Loos,
> When you were on the booze, as everybody knows.
> You stole the wenches, when I was in the trenches
> Facing an angry foe.
> You were a-slacking, when I was a-whacking
> The Huns on the Guillemont road ...

Oddly, the periods of world war in Belfast diminished the sectarian bitterness for a time, the adversaries finding a common purpose against a greater antagonist. Certainly once the aerial Blitz was over, there was a time of relative harmony. In the novel there is only minimal reference to the sectarian evil in the city, now relatively quiescent. When Frankie visits Simon Clarke on the Protestant Shankill Road, he flies past the gables covered with such earnest wishes as 'To hell with the Pope' but is reassured by Simon's advice, which he does not really understand:

> Frankie, don't you worry about the Pope. The Pope would give all the Irish tears for a smile from England.

One of his few Catholic colleagues is allowed a verbal attack on the most obvious adversary on the 'other side':

> That's the curse of Belfast. You could be a full cousin of the Pope or a half brother of the Duke of Norfolk – all these people are influential and powerful, but if they lived in Ulster, a farm labourer who happened to be chairman of Ballydoodle Orange Lodge would have ten times as much power as them.

In fact, when the book was being written and for at least a decade after its publication, there seemed to be a new spirit of tolerance abroad and anyone prophesying the carnage that followed after 1968 would have been scorned as a Cassandra.

The resurgent IRA campaign, 'Operation Harvest' (1956–62), had proved a failure, making little impact in the city, though it did provide the source of shipyard trouble that forged the theme of Sam Thompson's play *Over the Bridge* (1960). In fact the Frankies of the time were more likely to be troubled by their own side.

The character of Simon Clarke with his 'a plague o' both your houses' stance stands for reason amid a miasma of suspicion and religious hypocrisy:

> I'm doing a bit of gilding, Frankie – a church notice-board. Some minister or other has got a new degree conferred on him. He proved Luther was right in something he said, and wrote a book about it, so this is what he gets for it; more letters after his name … Some Catholic will write a book proving Luther was wrong and some school of learning will add letters to his name for it, just as some Protestant will say Luther was right and get letters after his too. Have you ever thought about this city you're living in, Frankie? Of the ghettoes in it? The Protestants are stuck in one district; the Catholics in another, the Jews somewhere else … The creeds and classes have made the place a bloody purgatory for themselves. But you're only a child with no head for that kind of talk. As you get older, talk to me and I'll put you wise about a few things in life to avoid, only don't ask me the point of living life as we do in Belfast.

At the weekly confraternity (at the Redemptorist monastery of Clonard, though not named) that Frankie is forced to attend, he notices that the priest 'nearly always talked about sin'. The prefect of the group to which he belongs is more of a snoop than a leader: 'Sally Blair's father had called him a "religious informer". It was said he was in everything connected with the church except the crib at Christmas' – a common gibe at those whose piety was unduly manifest. Tomelty was a believer and valued the strength, pattern and consolation that religion gave to wearied lives. He knew that properly accepted and practised it could be a worthwhile way of life but he was only too aware of the perversions that its authoritarian structure often led to. And he knew how lethal its mixture with politics could be. He wrote with great insight, empathy and humour about the priestly vocation in such plays as *Is the Priest at Home?* and its sequel *A Year at Marlfield* but he knew that fatigue, laziness, condescension, cowardice and even concupiscence were as much a part of the clergy's life as that of their flocks. He was also acutely conscious of the vast ignorance about the other side that each of the tribes betrayed. Kindness was to him much more important than piety; indeed he was certain the latter could not exist without the former. Yet in the city in which he lived, few seemed to understand this fundamental principle of Christianity. The history of city and province since those times has unfortunately borne out the implicit warning in his work about Ulster ancestral voices prophesying war. Yet it was no part of his mission in writing to preach. The warning was there for those who could read it.

The novel achieves its sociological purpose of presenting its time and its people in a light-hearted way including the slang, suspicions and urban myths of the period: at a dance the pianist/ MC announces, 'As there are not enough men as yet in the hall, there will be no objection to "Stagging" in the meantime; so, ladies and gentlemen get swinging to the strains of "I'll See You in My Dreams".' The orchestra was that of Tommy M'Fetridge and the Rhythm Kings, who reappeared as Majesty in *April in Assagh* that same year. And 'The Old Maid's Serenade to the Soldier', the bawdy song strongly disapproved of in *Mugs and Money*, also in 1953, has its first naughty line given in the text. A parody of 'Mother Machree' (1910), the most famous of all the transatlantic tear-jerkers by Rida Johnson Young (1865–1926), begins: 'Shure I love the brass buttons that shine on your spare … ' When it is discovered that the flamboyant Haig has had a divorce, his standing with the other painters increases because they associate divorce with the upper classes. Some, however, dismiss him as 'Rudolph

Vaselino', a gibe referring to the famous silent screen star who died in 1926. There is a rooted belief that hotel kitchens are dens of malpractice:

> I'll give him my share of hotels. I worked in one and we happened to be doing the kitchen apartments. There wasn't a bloody scrap of meat left on the plate that wasn't brought back to the kitchen and dumped into what they called the 'stock-pot'.

In *Red is the Port Light* Tomelty delivered a novel of great documentary authenticity even though he had never been a merchant seaman. With *The Apprentice* he writes from absolute experience about the craft of decorating, from both family and personal experience. He too suffered agonies because of a youthful stammer. His attempt at Mark Antony's 'Friends, Romans, countrymen' speech from *Julius Caesar* (III: ii), with the unassailable repeated initial 'F', gave rise to particular mockery and humiliation. However, compared to Frankie Price, his creator grew in confidence and became a gentle giant, tall, strong and fearless. What they had in common was a trade and it was a trade shared by two other literary Irishmen, who barely reached their forties: Brendan Behan (1923–1964) and Robert Noonan (1870–1911), using a homonym from the trade as his pseudonym, Robert Tressell, whose novel *The Ragged-Trousered Philanthropists* (1914) blew the whistle on the rapacity of employers and the skiving of the workmen, and remains a kind of holy writ for those caught in the class war. The attitudes and preoccupations of Frankie's workmates are also present at greater if more stately length in the novel.

The interesting and rather unusual thing about the novel is that it details the actual work done, with preparations of the sites before paint, distemper and paper are applied and the difficulties that high ceilings present, especially to those with poor balance:

> Frankie slid to his knees, pushed his feet over the plank and groped wildly for the rung of the ladder. Toby's hand gripped

the back of his overalls again. 'Come on,' Toby coaxed, 'you needn't be afraid. I've got a good grip of you, you won't fall. Take it easy for a minute or so when you get to the ground.' ... Painters were the only tradesmen who had to work from ready-made and insecure scaffolding.

Frankie, as the apprentice, has to do the most menial jobs but his seniors are, considering his ineptitude and his 'being one of *them*', in their rough way, supportive and his pride in having served (or survived) his apprenticeship is real and begins at last to increase his fragmented self-confidence. It shows in his preferring to bide among other postulants at the gates of the shipyard, the daily hiring-fair for casual workers, rather than accept the cushy job offered, as he rightly suspects, out of kindness, by Syl Haig. There is a hint here of the author's own pride in his trade skills.

Reading both the novels one realises that the dialogue of the characters, however crude, has a liveliness and an authenticity that could only have come from an author of great affinity with his creations, with an accurate ear for the speech patterns both of his birthplace and his adopted city. In fact his characters' chat is livelier and essentially more dramatic than the usual repetitive, disconnected, neutral pattern of ordinary conversations. His characters speak, though with no feeling of affectation, as they would sound on the stage, the dramatist's ear precisely tuned to what works histrionically. It was not until Harold Pinter devised a dramatically viable, equally contrived, locution that was closer to the broken-backed, wary, self-concealing nature of most oral communication, that one could dispense with 'realistic' dialogue. This ear for demotic speech rendered for dramatic transmission received its apotheosis in the remarkable radio series, *The McCooeys*.

The mark of the true artist is the confident way in which s/he takes risks. No one would have expected a *Bildungsroman* set in Belfast in the 1930s (a much lower and more dishonest decade than Auden ever dreamed) with an apparently hopeless hero to

have succeeded either in psychological or literary terms. Yet as
we leave the benighted Frankie safe in the ever-tightening arms
of Molly, we must admire the coup that Tomelty brought off. He
risked both the shoals of sentimentality and the reefs of despair
to write entertainingly and tenderly of a character who becomes a
hero with no heroic qualities. He has done more: the racked city
is allowed to redeem itself. A nun swathed in the contemporary
habit of tunic, guimp and veil, relives her childhood as she listens
to Toby sing as he works:

> I listened to you, and for a moment I thought I was back in my
> father's kitchen. That was a great song of his. It's remarkable
> that a whiff of a song can puff back the years like the wind
> skimming back the pages of a book.

Here and there the intermittently gloomy account of Frankie's
career is broken with thin shafts of brief sunlight. His joyless
adolescence is occasionally alleviated by the kindness of Sally
Blair, the child of kinder and more liberal parents, but the
inevitable hopeless yearning that follows the sharing of sweets
and chips makes his loneliness all the more poignant.

Tomelty was a man of deep feelings, stirred to rage and pity at
what he regarded as unnecessary poverty, the bullying, whether
of rooted officialdom or the petty little bosses in the workplace,
the sense of lost nationality in the Catholic people of Ulster and
the joylessness of much of the life lived by his fellow citizens. Yet
there is still, even in the black city, the possibility of pleasure,
romance, at least for the young and if not happiness then a settled
low content for the rest. A loving couple crosses the road, 'their
movements suggesting a slow waltz'. In the street where Frankie
spent his abominable childhood and adolescence, young people
'passed on with dancing-shoes under their arms or steel-ridged
skating boots'. In spite of religious demarcation the city is still a
living entity and has the will to survive. It may be two cities, each
with its own *modus vivendi* but with the capacity to seek life,

liberty and happiness. A pity that they could not engage with each other. *The Apprentice* is neither tract nor manifesto but it is an implicit plea that the comedian James Young (1918–74), in a sense created by *The McCooeys*, kept urging in later programmes: 'Will yes stop fightin'.' Whatever the book may tell us of Frankie Price and his times it is a great, unwitting tribute to the kindness and geniality of his creator.

By the time the novel was published Tomelty was at the height of his powers. He had a full-time film career, was writing weekly radio scripts for *The McCooeys*, and had nearly completed *Is the Priest at Home?*, his most popular play. As his friend David Kennedy put it, the desire to move 'away from the confining bonds of realism' meant that *The Apprentice* was his last major prose work and served as a testament to his own past and a kind of exorcism of boyhood demons.

14

The McCooeys

NE DAY IN THE EARLY 1950s, Henry McMullan, Director of Programmes in BBC Northern Ireland, received a telephone call from Lord Brookeborough, the Prime Minister of Northern Ireland, asking him as a personal favour to postpone till a later time the broadcast of the intensely popular radio programme, *The McCooeys*, because his kitchen staff refused to think about serving dinner until it was over. Sam Hanna Bell, who first suggested Tomelty as scriptwriter, reported that once, preparing for an outside broadcast on a summer Saturday evening, he walked down a street in Waterfoot on the Antrim Coast and every single radio was tuned to Ormeau Avenue because Bobby Greer, the grocer, or Granda McCooey, or Derek, the window cleaner, was in full flow. He was able to follow the whole episode as to 'what the McCooeys and their neighbours had been up to by the time you reached the little bridge at the village's end'. It was heard every week from 1949 until 1954 with a repeat on the following Monday, and required a prodigious amount of writing, to say nothing of the development of storylines and the introduction of new and gripping characters. It was the most popular radio programme ever aired by BBC Northern Ireland, listener research discovering an audience of half a million, which, considering the population of Northern Ireland at the time was about 1.6 million, meant that one in three adults were fans.

The idea was first suggested to McMullan by the Controller, Andrew Carpenter, once Director of Programmes in Scotland, opining that a series about an ordinary Belfast family might have the same success on BBC Northern Ireland as a similar series called *The McFlannels* had in Scotland. Bell was consulted by Carpenter and without hesitation he nominated Tomelty as the perfect writer for the concept. As Bell reported in the *Ulster Tatler* profile, he was asked to take Tomelty to lunch at the Grosvenor Rooms to put the proposition to him and took 'Pastor' Boyd along as an extra voice in the discussion. Bell had brought with him two of the *McFlannels* books already published but Tomelty waved them aside. As Bell put it in the piece: 'If a radio family were to be created they would be drawn from the author's knowledge of the quiddity of people, with an ear and an eye alert to every turn of speech and gesture.'

BBC Northern Ireland had a problem that BBC Scotland did not have to face, the tribal nature of the city. In the 800,000 words that followed there was not a hint of either politics or religion; it pleased the Northern Ireland controllers though some later commentators have seen this as evidence of cowardice on the part of the author. It was, in fact, a feat of brilliant literary contrivance and greatly increased its popularity. Tomelty had shown that he could do politics and religion as well as the next braggart, and listeners on both sides of the divide believed the series spoke for them. Granda and Aunt Sarah were probably the most popular characters, though Tomelty himself, as the lugubrious grocer Bobby Greer, who was a laggard in love in his wooing of Aunt Sarah, was the best known for his frequent admonition, 'Schlup up yer shloup.'

It re-oriented the stage career of James Young, who, having been the original Willie John of the *Barnum* plays and achieved great fame as Derek the window cleaner, reappeared in a series of sketches in his own shows, as 'Orange Lil' and the 'Cherryvalley Lady'. He had been the ghost of Stephen in *All Souls' Night* and was George to Tomelty's Lennie in *Of Mice and Men*, regarded as one of the finest of the UGT's productions. Booked to do a short sketch in a midnight matinee in the Ritz cinema, he asked Tomelty to provide the script. It was a great success and persuaded Young to take the comedy route. Sadly he, too, was one of the defectors after Tomelty's accident. Derek's knowing, 'Oh now … ' joined 'You're a comeedjan', 'Shloup wih vegabittles' and (offering cigarettes) 'Have one; have two; have the whole packet!' to become a universal part of Belfast conversation. The characters assumed a reality more colourful than the often drab lives of some of the listeners. Min Milligan was advised by letter not to have anything more to do with Greer and to meet the correspondent at the Albert Clock with a view to matrimony. When the family had the decorators in, they were chided for not getting an estimate of the cost beforehand and were given advice about the best kind of wallpaper. The city bus manager wrote to the BBC to ask the McCooeys not to keep on complaining about the necessary rise in fares. And one member of the cast was to receive international fame: Stephen Boyd (né Billy Millar) later found stardom in Hollywood but is remembered as the detective who was 'just making one or two enquiries'.

The scripts were typed on Tomelty's old portable typewriter in his usual single-finger style while the necessary cigarette reeked in the other hand. A single script covered fourteen foolscap pages and at times they were conceived under extreme circumstances because of theatre and cinema commitments. Once, during the filming of the studio shots for *Hell Below Zero*, he was commanded to stay in London by the director Mark Robson (1913–78), sore that he could not accompany the star Alan Ladd on a projected outing to Paris. To Tomelty's consternation, he remembered that he had written himself into the script for the episode to be recorded on the Saturday. He travelled by overnight train to Glasgow, caught a plane to Nutts Corner, arriving at Ormeau Avenue at noon in time for the recording. He was back in London that night, thus avoiding Robson's wrath.

The McCooeys was an unmissable date for the province and beyond. It appealed to all ages and it was a regular date for Roma and Frances, who, after their baths on a Saturday evening, sat in their nightdresses, their hair done up in papers. Being the daughters and granddaughters of two famous actors, they took in their stride. As Daddy and Granny usually reminded people, they were *in* the theatre but not *of* it. After the sports reports, the signature tune of the programme, an arrangement of the popular Belfast tune 'My Aunt Jane' by David Curry, introduced another feast of fun and acutely observed family life. For those over sixty the memory remains a whiff of a lost golden age and even now the glory has not departed. It is what Tomelty is mainly remembered for, its richness and entertainment value tending to occlude more lasting works. Some friends felt that the scriptwriting was an ill-advised waste of artistic talent but it was excellent of its kind; as the March Hare might have put it, 'The very best butter.'

15
Priest-Ridden?

A S I HAVE SUGGESTED MORE THAN once, Tomelty was a man of deep feelings, stirred to rage and pity at what he regarded as unnecessary poverty, bullying, whether arising out of rooted officialdom or the petty little bosses in the workplace, the sense of lost nationality and alienation among the Catholic people of Ulster and the joylessness of much of the life lived by his contemporaries. His work in the 'dark' plays, as I have dubbed them, was partly expository and partly exorcist. They were written too with hope of gaining sympathy for the weak and poor, and as a challenge to those whose duty it might be in a position to ameliorate their condition. He identified, not always vicariously, with the misery of unemployment and dead-end jobs in the city, and the dangerous struggle for existence among the fishermen and deckhands of his native Strangford Lough. As with all the serious literature of the period, his work becomes an appeal for the kind of central state support that Attlee's government were to bring in after the 1945 election. It also makes a plea for absolution for those who, driven by want and drabness, were led to commit the venial sins of the poor.

Yet he was not addicted to gloom but had a temperament rather like that of Oliver Edwards, the friend of Dr Johnson, who said: 'I have tried too in my time to be a philosopher, but I don't know how, cheerfulness was always breaking in.' Tomelty's natural ebullience continued to surface in his life as in his art; the festiveness of being he considered of prime importance and any anger he showed in his work was directed at those who would deprive people of this right. As often in Irish literature, the comic becomes a more appropriate and more subtle medium than the tragic in such cases. His primary aim was entertainment but the underlining of his moral purpose with humour was as effective, if not more so, than in *The End House* and the novels. The lad who had left school at twelve was now as confident and as effective an artist as the graduate friends whom he may once have envied. He had such a rich imagination and way with words in dialogue, characterisation and authentic locutions, that the temptation ever so slightly to over-egg the gloom and misery in those powerful writings was hard to resist.

As an actor and theatre professional, he was acutely aware of how a character could be portrayed, as a writer he had the gift of conveying a picture in words and as a dramatist, an exact ear for dialogue, especially of the speech of Belfast and his native region of County Down. These qualities are even more essential to the writer of comedies than starker 'serious' plays. Just as comedy is a tougher prospect for amateurs, so artifice and technique play a larger part in the light than the dark. Apart from *All Souls' Night* and *The End House*, Tomelty's plays have tended to be at least 'comedic' but none the less effective for that.

Is the Priest at Home? (1954), a gently comic account of the life of a tolerant curate in a new parish, was Tomelty's longest-running play. Father Malan is beset on the one side by the offstage Canon and on the other by the gang of lay enthusiasts, from GAA activists to 'holy Joes' who would presume to teach him his trade. The Catholic Church is believed to have been changed radically in the half-century since the play was written but parish life has essentially changed very little. There may be an absence of worshippers aged 20–50 but the priest is still expected to be at home when he may be needed. Its unstated 'message' is that the Ireland of the 1950s, assumed by modern historians to have been priest-ridden and the Church structures superficially at their strongest, was a rather more complicated country. And the 'Wee North' had the extra, potentially turbulent, element of sectarianism.

The play is 'comic' in the sense that the plays of Chekhov are comic, in the fact that there are no major tragedies, few, if any, violent deaths but just people leading lives of quiet desperation. The debate about clerical power is introduced a little clumsily by an induction scene using only a table and a single spot, involving a visiting American who is allowed to question the priest about the details of his calling: 'I'd like to talk – really talk – to one of you Irish priests. I'd just like to know how you get on top … Rome says you must do this and that … and buddy they gotta do it.' The priest responds meekly: 'I wish you were right,' and the three acts that follow demonstrate that the assumption that priests have 'the screws on the folks' is far from right. The part of the priest was played by Harold Goldblatt. It is possible that the author and the director (Goldblatt himself) wanted to make a non-vocal comment on his perceived nonconformity by the fixed – not to say smug – attitudes of the Irish Church of the time. By 1954 the Group company had reached a standard of ensemble acting that was better than the average British rep. Goldblatt, Devlin, Margaret D'Arcy, Patrick McAlinney and James Ellis were beginning to get offers to appear on television, while the author was already launched as a leading character actor in films.

Jimmy the 'Curate' explains his title and his position in an early speech:

You see I've been knocking about here for the past thirty years – cleaning the church, digging graves, lighting the lights, counting the collections, looking after the baptismal register, caretaker of what we have for a hall … putting on concerts … holding the box for St Vincent de Paul … And generally making myself useful about the place.

Later in Act III he reveals that he was once a seminarian himself until he was put off by the casually offensive remarks of 'a snob of a secular priest'. In a sense he is a modern version of the bright servant of seventeenth- and eighteenth-century drama who, smarter, freer and more resourceful than his master, contrives to get him out of scrapes. And in this play his chief dramatic purpose is to explain the intricacy of relationships in the Catholic parish of Marlfield to the new curate, to help him distinguish in his ministry between Cathal McNulty, the local GAA fanatic (causing Marona, his wry housekeeper, to wonder if the abbreviation should be pronounced 'G Ah Ah' or 'G Ay Ay'), who is also the 'head of Catholic Action' in the parish, and the local socialist Karl Marx O'Grady who, with his 'progressive' coterie in a part of town known as the Kremlin, parrots communist holy writ, supports soccer rather than Gaelic but, as Marona admits, he and his fellow progressives spend their time ' … writing away for pensions for you and the like. And now they are trying to get water in all the houses and flush closets. Imagine that!'

Tomelty had a retentive ear for Ulster idiom and used to devise new examples himself. Marona, fed up with Jimmy's fussing, rounds on him in dialect: 'Aren't you the sore oul' gulshin' for asking questions?' Discovering dry rot in the study, Jimmy decides to warn the priest to keep any furniture 'a beagle's gowl away'. These were – and are – common Ulster expressions and ones that would have delighted audiences province-wide. But Jimmy's description of his temporary mending of the dry rot hole as 'I was just fixing a bit of tin over a wee discrepancy in the floor' was original yet recognisably appropriate to the ears of the audience.

To maintain the priority of humour and public entertainment in his play, Tomelty indulged himself in an in-joke. The previous incumbent, Fr Greer, had been transferred to the region of Tomelty's birth and boyhood but Marona was not willing to go with him: 'He's gone down to the Ards country. And I heard other priests saying it was like the foreign missions down there … ' Earlier priests are discussed by Jimmy:

> During the war we had a curate here, Father Diamond, and he was heart and soul with the Savings Certificates, the Red Cross, and he had my back nearly broken collecting wastepaper for the war effort. He, I must say, went down well with the other sort. But our own ones didn't like him. They called him a West Briton.

The 'other sort' of whichever digging foot could hardly be ignored in a naturalistic Ulster play (a fact that makes the writing of The McCooeys such a feat of dramatic skill). When Malan asks Jimmy about the existence of sectarian trouble he assures him: 'None, Father, none at all. There may be a bit of fuss around the Twelfth, but that's only to be expected.' Incidents of the sort are minor, even trivial. The local vet displayed orange lilies and a drunken Catholic farmer tried to pull them down. The crisis vanished when the farmer's wife had to send for the vet when one of his cows calved … 'so all was forgotten'.

Malan's immediate predecessor was different from Fr Diamond: ' … quite the reverse. Nothing for him but the GAA. No English dances or anything of that kind. The soccer crowd … didn't like him at all.' Small Ulster town struggles: after a spiritual retreat and a promise made to the 'missioner' (the order priest who did the preaching) that the parish would stop taking the News of the World, the only two newsagents in the town – both Catholic – stopped stocking the paper, notorious then for its detailed court-case reports and famous for its excellent sports coverage, and so their 'other sort' had to go elsewhere:

... they got their own back. When the Canon thought he would
have pictures on Sunday nights in the hall, they got round the
local county councillors to vote against a seven-day licence for
the hall. You'll find in the North, Father, that Calvinism affects
Catholicism, just as Catholicism affects Calvinism.

These kind of tensions in a place where ' ... the Catholics are
in the majority in the village itself, but the outlying country places
are mostly Protestant, except the mountain district' were in those
years relatively harmless but the capacity for and the actual
possibility of communal violence was intuited by a man of
Tomelty's sensitivity. It was not, however, *his* intention to thunder
or prescribe. He could not avoid the reality of Ulster but chose
rather to portray for his audiences, through his art, the nature of
their society, and in this play his purpose was to please the public
and to have them consider the real nature of the priest in his parish.
It was an imaginative portrait with inside information from priest
friends and fairly refuted the American's insistence that the priest
had the 'screws on the folks'. The last word in the matter is given
inevitably to Jimmy the 'Curate': 'They tell you that the country's
priest-ridden. I'm thinking it's the other way around – that the
priest is people-ridden.'

The audience who watched as Perpetua O'Kane, wife of the
owner of 'the general grocery, coal and produce store on the
Market Square', sister of Monsignor Macklin ('You wouldn't know
my brother, Monsignor Macklin ... He's on the South American
mission ... '), and chief gossip in a town riddled with backbiting,
tries to inveigle herself into the position of lay power that she
held with the previous incumbent, would have recognised her
instantly. Fr Malan begins to realise what a formidable adversary
she could be as Jimmy lists her roles of parish involvement:

> Always remember that O'Kane has a good deal of parochial
> power. She's head Child of Mary in the parish. She's president
> of the Legion of Mary. She's head bombardier of the Ladies of
> Charity. President of the Altar Society. Secretary of the Sacred

Heart Sodality. Chief of the Library. And further, don't forget she has the ear of the Canon.

That last office was not insignificant; it was not unknown for the local librarian to act as a kind of censor, refusing to allow the work of 'immoral' writers on their shelves. One example of an 'immoral' writer of the time was Somerset Maugham, as a County Down friend of mine discovered when he suggested to his local librarian that she should order his novel *Cakes and Ale* and received a hot sermon from the vexed guardian of public virtue.

Tomelty very cleverly delineates the minefield that a mildly liberal priest had to traverse in that period of vaunted public morality. Everything was so clear-cut in those pre-Vatican II Church Militant days. Even the social legislation that led to the founding of the NHS was frowned on by those who could afford to pay for private health treatment and when one of Malan's sermons seems to praise it, his words are vociferously disapproved of by the local chemist and his daughter. He is forced to balance the needs and rights of all his flock but comes down heavily and justly on a boycott instituted by the local pious bullies on a local drunken shopkeeper. The shopkeeper is somewhat feckless, with many children, an empty-headed wife and a problem with the Church's teaching on contraception, and his shop is placed out of bounds because of a fracas in which he is thought to have deliberately injured the priest. The savagery of such a boycott was seen a few years later in Fethard-on-Sea in County Wexford when Protestant businessmen and professionals were subject to a boycott by Catholics under the instructions of their local priest. It was not the Church's finest hour as the damage to the life of the town became clear.

The effect of its authenticity was to make the play the most popular of all Tomelty's work, frequently revived until the 'Soggarth Aroon' as a character slipped out of relevance in Irish drama. Audiences would also have recognised the other essentially stock characters that formed the personae of Ulster – and, indeed, general Irish – plays because they were, with a little artistic licence, faithful representations of the parish people they knew, whether in city or hamlet. They were not pilloried as fools or villains but seen as what Falstaff inclusively called 'mortal men'. The 'Curate' might not have been recognised as a stock character – there was too much ingenuity and originality in his creation – but Marona, the no-nonsense priest's housekeeper, was immediately identifiable with, however, few of the mythological powers of influence, even control, ascribed to the species. The type had figured before and would figure later in Irish drama.

Tomelty's skill was to take recognisable types and, giving them individual life, use them for his double purpose of entertainment and subliminal instruction. On the opening night on Tuesday, 18 May 1954, when the author appeared in response to the usual cries of 'Author! Author!' he suggested, as reported by the *Northern Whig* on 19 May, that a play 'in which we were able to see the other fellow's point was a type of play needed in a community such as ours. He would like to see more plays of this kind.' The newspaper assented, commenting that 'Most people who see this production are likely to agree with him.' Other press responses were favourable; the *Belfast News Letter* on the same date asserted that the 'priest had been raised from his theatrical rut' and that Fr Malan continues to be 'disturbed by the self-righteous façade of religion and the narrow politico-religious bigotry, which he encounters ... '; in *Ireland's Saturday Night* on the following weekend, 'Prospero', the theatre critic, talked of 'Tomelty's bathyscaphe' – the instrument for deep-sea observation: ' ... if he can't be said to have reached the bottom of his chosen social problem at least [he] gets well below the surface ... ' The Dublin-based *Standard* of 11 June, having seen the play in the Abbey, found it 'brimful of laugh-camouflaged social criticism and teaching as many lessons as a Lent-full of sermons ... deserves to be seen in every town and village in Ireland'. The Dublin *Evening Mail* applauded the way the play 'answers the accusation that Ireland is a priest-ridden country and there is something delicious in a man from Belfast being the one to deal with that delicate question. Yet Joseph Tomelty has done it safely and in the doing he has performed the feat of making us laugh at ourselves'.

The dramatic originality of the character of Fr Malan was that he was ordinary – not tormented like the priests in *Shadow and Substance* by Paul Vincent Carroll and *The Righteous are Bold* by Frank Carney. The theme of the priest beset by his flock rather than the reverse Tomelty got from the experiences of Lena and her friend Ellie in parish work in St Peter's. It was the first Irish play to mention birth control or hint at abortion and domestic violence. It was condemned from many a rural pulpit with the result that many a priest went to see it in disguise or watched it from the wings. The prelude and coda were deliberately set in a thinly disguised Wynn's Hotel in Dublin, a place popular with priests and frequented by Tomelty himself. The author gave special permission for a production by the clerical students of the Irish College in Rome, with the part of Marona played by Patrick Walsh, later Bishop of Down and Connor.

The charge that Ireland was then priest-ridden was subtly disproved, at least in the case of Father Malan, though the questing American brought on in a coda remained unconvinced. The role of all Churches in western democracies, like most other things in an imperfect world, is a complicated one; a balance between the sacred and the profane, the terrestrial and the celestial. The condition of post-lapsarian creatures with earthly instincts and heavenly ambitions is bound to be unstable, and that description includes priests and bishops. Mortal men and very human clerics. The play ends without a neat dramatic resolution; life and the struggle go on – and we must be satisfied.

16
Fine Frenzy

A
S MENTIONED EARLIER, DAVID KENNEDY, IN
two summaries of Tomelty's work, in *The Arts in Ulster*
(1951) and *Rann* (1953), noted a slight shift in his dramatic
work, arising perhaps out of an impatience with realistic plays or a
surfeit of that kind of writing when having to prepare the scripts
for *The McCooeys*. Kennedy did not necessarily approve of the
change but merely noted the evidence for it. He talked of
Tomelty's desire to move 'away from the confining bonds of
realism which may prove to be his most valuable contribution to
the theatre'. Tomelty had, of course, shown his mastery of
naturalistic comedy in the *Barnum* plays, his capacity as a social
commentator with *The End House* and his sensitive picture of
the clerical vocation in *Is the Priest at Home? Idolatry at
Innishargie* toyed with fantasy and there were fantastic elements
blithely incorporated in *All Souls' Night*. His basic literary cosmos
and his new departure could, with a little forcing, be summed up
by Theseus's speech in Shakespeare's *A Midsummer Night's
Dream*:

The lunatic, the lover and the poet
Are of imagination all compact:
One sees more devils than vast hell can hold,
That is the madman; the lover, all as frantic,
Sees Helen's beauty in a brow of Egypt:
The poet's eye, in a fine frenzy rolling,
Doth glance from heaven to earth, from earth to heaven;
And as imagination bodies forth
The forms of things unknown, the poet's pen
Turns them to shapes and gives to airy nothing
A local habitation and a name.

By 1953, Tomelty had taken comedy and naturalistic drama as far as he thought he could. *Down the Heather Glen* (1953), first staged in the Belfast Arts Theatre, is a play hard to categorise: black comedy, modern morality, folk drama? Perhaps a little of each. In 'the seat of a glen on an island somewhere off the North East coast of Ireland' there is a play toward. The place is intended as a symbol for the Ireland of the time where, as one of the characters states in an inversion of St Paul, it is God who goes about like a roaring lion. In general there is not enough devilment about. The play is a version of Sophocles' *Oedipus Rex* and its basic theme of classical incest is at once a deliberate protest against the Puritanism and the venality that characterises the island community.

The people's morals are sedulously guarded by M'Master who, with a son, Hugh, and Bain, a deputy, is determined to prevent any modernistic ideas from polluting the island's sanctity. They hold the threat of the Law and the Church over the people but the ultimate chilling sanction is incarceration in the mental hospital in Downpatrick. It is not a generous creed since it is based on stasis and money-grubbing and the symbol of its continuity will be sanctified in the marriage of Hugh and Rebecca, Bain's daughter. In the second act the audience is given a glimpse of what that marriage will be like since their courtship consists almost entirely of monetary and territorial concerns. Opposition to the choking piety of the place is provided by Gerald, who is intent upon staging the play even though M'Master and Bain outwit him at every point. Even their open-air rehearsal is baulked by a lack of oil since the dealer obeys the instruction not to sell. They manage to turn the wives of two of the main actors against the project and the third, having failed to woo Babs, the daughter of a local grandee, leaves the island. Significantly named Tom, Dick and Harry, their singing of the song of the play's title, once an anthem of defiance, ceases to sound.

A certain Satanic element is prepared for in the talk of Sebina (a name Tomelty used before in *Idolatry in Innishargie*), one of Gerald's few allies, who is known to speak well of Lucifer. As in *Idolatry* a coffin-shaped box is brought in from the sea and suddenly, out of the cave placed centre stage, comes the Professor, bringing with him at least an intellectual whiff of brimstone. He has much to say about contemporary Ireland: ' ... if there's a country in the world with less love in it than Ireland, I'd like to visit it.' Gerald agrees, adding: ' ... there's more bunk talked about the love of the Irish mother. Nine out of every ten of them are as greedy as Ananias. They chase their childer away from them to where they'll earn the most money and won't worry how the hell they are living as long as there's a chapel or a church near to where they stay.' There is much more of this subversive talk of the sort that might be denounced as Gerald says: ' ... like a mad missioner raving about hell'.

In spite of recurring gloom, the play has many moments of hilarity. The rehearsal and discussion of parts owe something to the scenes with the 'rude mechanicals' in the *Dream*, and the Professor has many good lines. There is one neat in-joke as Gerald summarises critically the main fare of the Group:

> ... folks in Ulster wouldn't give a hearing to my play. Aren't they forever flocking in their thousands to plays about moiley cows, and the clumsy courtin' of clarts in a kitchen – not to mention the fingering of figures in a will or the fistlis of fools on a fair day.

Gerald and the trio speak occasionally in verse, often in rhyme ('Afore you take me by the throat,/Is sin not the lining of grace's coat?') and at times either in homage to Synge or O'Casey or in mild parody, language is deliberately strained: 'Am I to stand as a scarecrow while he searches my throat for my Adam's apple to twist it as he pleases?'

In spite of its comic elements and deliberate artificialities of language, the play's purpose is serious, even angry. It also shows a new confidence on the part of its creator in handling the new and, if necessary, the bizarre but it must have confused many whose only experience of Tomelty's work was in the *Barnum* plays. Yet on closer examination it becomes clear that elements of strangeness had already begun to appear in such plays as *All Souls' Night* and *Idolatry at Innishargie*. The artist's palette had certain primary colours that he used often. One of the more comic moments occurs when discussing material for making the Greek robes for *Oedipus*. Gerald, Harry, Tom and Sebina all admit they can produce fine coloured material for the purpose, all found in that traditional way. There too is given the best excuse yet for gathering prog from foundered ships: 'Is it thievin' to fight the sea to curb its greed?' As a play it could not have been anything as popular as the other works but it is a fascinating piece of work for all that.

It is certain that Tomelty's wide reading would have included the plays of Lady Gregory that had such an influence on W.B. Yeats and the early Abbey Theatre. *The Rising of the Moon* (1907) remains her most popular piece but a play written three years earlier was just as influential. This was *Spreading the News*, a comedy about how easily rumour can possess a town. In the play, Jack Smith forgets a hayfork and the villagers of Cloon see Bartley Fallon rush after him to return it and as gossip spreads he finds himself in danger of arrest for Smith's murder. With Tomelty the village is Assagh which figures in four of his later plays and in each case the temper of the mob is roused by false intelligence.

The Drunken Sailor (1954) – another play with a song as title –
was written for radio and is essentially a work for voices.

Assagh seems to have been his own invention but it serves like
Brian Friel's Ballybeg as the author's Everytown. (Its Gaelic
homophone *easach* means 'waterfall'). The play opens in the
village's only pub where the first speaker, Sylvester Brannigan,
calls for drink for 'a disturbed sailor'. The landlord Ballafer (a
name used that same year in *Is the Priest at Home?*), suspecting
trouble, is at first reluctant to serve him and eventually shows
him the door. Sylvester is reluctant to join his ship in spite of
being summoned personally by a fellow crew-member. His
drinking companion is a philosophical gravedigger who acts as a
kind of detached chorus throughout. After his eviction from the
pub Sylvester acts as 'bottler' (money collector) for an itinerant
street musician whose offerings change from 'The Bold Fenian
Men' to 'The Sash My Father Wore' in the appropriate part of
town, especially near Ballafer's pub: 'He's what's known as a
religious Orangeman. That, in these parts, is a terror.' The pair
have no luck in collecting cash because already the village children
are singing 'What shall we do with the drunken sailor?' and the
crescendo of voices builds up the fear: 'He's left his good ship
and he's wandering about with a knife ... My man says he heard
the Sailor was a Red Russian.' Later the voices call him 'a mad
Spaniard', 'a Lascar', even a 'Chinaman' who 'knifed Bellafer'.

Even Lizzie Latimer, who once kept a dosshouse, is now too
grand because of Nye Bevan, for whom she has a higher regard
than St Patrick:

> I have new teeth. I have me specs for reading, writing and me
> 'Baritone' tablets for making me sleep. That's welfare for you.
> I'm sure of everything – only me passage to heaven – and you
> never know what another Labour Government will do. All free,
> gratis and for nothing.

Overnight all is changed when the (false) intelligence comes from Portaferry that Sylvester's ship is missing: ' ... one of her lifeboats was picked up near Kilclief' (a port on the Lecale peninsula south of Strangford). Immediately the voices change, they become sympathetic to the stranded mariner:

> God help the unfortunate ... There's a shilling. It's all I can afford ... There's half-a-crown. God knows, it's little enough ... I'm sure Smith the draper would give him a shirt ... And Brown the bootman a pair of boots ... We must do all we can for the crature, God help him.

Predictably they change yet again as the word comes that the ship is safe and Sylvester leaves town still in search of peace, repeating his mantra, *'Dona Nobis Pacem'*, and giving all the money he received to be shared by the gravedigger and the musician. For an exercise in cynicism and mob waywardness it is oddly moving.

The quintessence of Tomelty's humorous alternative theatre is to be found in *April in Assagh* which opened in the Grand Opera House on 13 December 1954. Its cast of twelve was a roll-call of the UGT greats. Tomelty himself played M'Greevy, the sane and sophisticated water engineer who eventually stills the rumour of plague that he unwittingly began. The rich variety of village archetypes included R.H. McCandless as George Killops, known as 'Pope' because of his unswerving uncritical support for the Catholic Church. His adversary 'Stalin' (Harry Burke) was played by J.G. Devlin, while the young James Ellis was Thomas M'Fetridge, a band leader known as 'Majesty' who had a walk-on part in the novel *The Apprentice*, and Maurice O'Callaghan was Jimmy Magee, who as a prisoner of war had memorised the text of an encyclopaedia and never quite recovered from his experiences. Known as 'Drop o'Tay' because of his mild addiction to caffeine, he is easily driven to long-memorised speeches from his book: 'Now, take Marie Antoinette. She said the people could have plenty of cake if they had no bread.' Snippets about Titus

Oates, Moses, the Borgias, Egyptian cats, the Nile, Martin Luther, and Valhallas are a constant part of 'Drop o'Tay's' manic conversation. Elizabeth McKeown, Elizabeth Begley, Irene Bingham, Catherine Gibson and Jean Lundy completed an all-star cast.

As his friend Sam Hanna Bell revealed in 1942, 'Joe has been reading Chekhov.' *April in Assagh* is his most Chekhovian play but it comes rather from the early 'vaudeville' period before Stanislavski darkened his work down. The title month is the one notoriously mercurial in temperament and as the play shuttles back and forth the mood changes from mockery to terror to farce. It begins with the loss of Lucinda's predatory cat Barney, about whose famous sexual career his elderly lady owner is unaware. An excellent hunter, he is suddenly in great demand because 'the schooner *Heligoland* wrecked herself Monday week, and her cargo of barley is spread on the beaches as far up as the highwater mark' and Barney is 'the best ratter round these parts'. The scene is set for unease, intensified by the April brightening and darkening of the sky. The water pump that is the village's main source of water has dried up and M'Greevy, the plumber, who also plays the church organ, is busy at a wedding. The rumour persists that the missing cat's body is in the pump and that all who drink it will die of plague.

Then the pet cat belonging to Miss Duff, who would like to be thought of as minor aristocracy, takes ill and a graver rumour starts that Seth Mulligan's milk is poisoned. The play continues with scare following upon scare like *Spreading the News* on speed and when the water pump is fixed, the sickness of Meser, Miss Duff's cat, proves to have been caused by birth pangs and, 'normality' restored, the sky darkens ominously, portending flood. It is a deliberately protracted comedy that permits the reasonable voice of the author, mediated through the character M'Greevy, a part that suited him perfectly, to excoriate the mores of his native province, of whatever religious or political grouping. One of his lines, quoted earlier, is heartfelt: 'I wish we had a plague of Religiosmyopia in Ulster for about ten years.'

One other significant play, written first for radio in 1948 and adapted for television in 1971, is almost without political or satirical overtones yet it is thoroughly representative of its author's genius. The title *The Singing Bird* comes from a popular parlour song from an old Munster air with lyrics by Edith Wheeler:

> I have seen the lark soar high at morn,
> Heard his song up in the blue.
> I have heard the blackbird pipe his note.
> The thrush and the linnet too,
> But there's none of them can sing so sweet,
> My singing bird as you.
>
> If I could lure my singing bird
> From his own cosy nest.
> If I could catch my singing bird
> I would warm him on my breast,
> For there's none of them can sing so sweet,
> My singing bird as you.

As will now be clear, music, especially song, played an important part in Tomelty's life. He was a fine singer himself, though it was his youngest brother Peter who took it up as a career and regularly visited Belfast to take lessons from the tenor James Johnston (1903–1991), the Belfast butcher who, encouraged by Tyrone Guthrie, became a star at Covent Garden. The idea of the predatory hawk came from an incident when Tomelty's wife had the heart of a small bird dropped at her feet by a raptor that had nested in one of the spires of St Peter's. The frail nature of Aneas Anketelle's grasp on sanity was a condition that continued to fascinate Tomelty and the presence of music and singing voices seemed as natural to him as the air he breathed – in fact was part of it. It is a play about kindness and tolerance and leaves the question unanswered as to how Aneas's drowned wife actually met her end. It is a kind of perfect radio play with church music and the voices, especially of singing children, a necessary part. With Tomelty in the lead in both productions, the television play filmed fifteen years after the accident, his performances are infinitely moving and the results lead to the conviction that *The Singing Bird* is his best short play and, with *All Souls' Night*, deserving of a permanent place in the canon of Irish literature.

At the Group, play unknown.

Backstage at the Group.

Possibly Friends and Relations *by St John Ervine at the Group. Tomelty is on the right.*

ABBEY THEATRE

THE NATIONAL THEATRE SOCIETY, LTD
LENNOX ROBINSON, RICHARD HAYES
ERNEST BLYTHE, ROIBEARD O'FARACHAIN
ERIC GORMAN

EASTER MONDAY at 8.15 p.m.

PERFORMANCE IN COMMEMORATION OF EASTER, 1916. (On the occasion
of the coming into force of the Republic of Ireland Act, 1948)

DERVORGILLA
A Tragedy in One Act, by LADY GREGORY

THE RISING OF THE MOON
A Play in One Act, by LADY GREGORY

LOST LIGHT
A Verse Play by ROIBEARD O'FARACHAIN

TUESDAY, 19th APRIL, 1949, and following nights at 7.45

ALL SOULS' NIGHT
A Play in Three Acts, by JOSEPH TOMELTY

LATECOMERS NOT ADMITTED UNTIL END OF FIRST ACT

Stalls, 5/-; Centre Balcony, 2/6; Side Balcony, 1/-; Pit, 3/-

ALL SEATS CAN BE RESERVED   BOX OFFICE 10.30 TO 6   PHONE 74505

ABBEY THEATRE

THE NATIONAL THEATRE SOCIETY, LTD
LENNOX ROBINSON, RICHARD HAYES
ERNEST BLYTHE, ROIBEARD O'FARACHAIN
ERIC GORMAN

MONDAY, 28th AUGUST, 1944
AND FOLLOWING NIGHTS AT 7.30.   DOORS OPEN AT 7

FIRST PRODUCTION OF

THE END HOUSE

A PLAY IN THREE ACTS, BY

JOSEPH TOMELTY

Doors Close before Rise of Curtain. Late-comers will NOT
be admitted until first interval.

PRICES : Stalls, 4/- & 3/-; Balcony, 2/6 & 1/-; Pit. 2/- & 1/6

ALL SEATS CAN BE RESERVED   BOX OFFICE 10.30 TO 6   PHONE 74505

Abbey posters.

As Boyd in Boyd's Shop *on BBC Television, Sheila Maughan is Agnes (right of Joe).*

Tomelty and Mrs. Jean Harvey from Carrickfergus in Legacy of Delight *by Hugh Quinn. Jean would go on to play The Widow from Carnlough in* The McCooeys.

THIS INDENTURE made the   day of   1942 BETWEEN
Harold Goldblatt of 22, Waterloo Gardens in the County of the City of
Belfast Director of the first part, Daniel Fitzpatrick of 18, Joy Street
Belfast aforesaid Merchant of the second part, Robert H. MacCandless of
"Braeside", North Road Carrickfergus in the County of Antrim Pharmaceutical
Chemist of the third part, James R. Mageean of 72, Eglantine Avenue Belfast
aforesaid Artist of the fourth part, P. Joseph Tomelty of 81, Iris Drive
Belfast aforesaid Manager of the fifty part, John O'Malley of 18, Vicarage
Park Belfast aforesaid Clerk of the sixth part, and John J. Moss of 27,
Chichester Street Belfast aforesaid Solicitor of the seventh part.
WITNESSETH that the said Harold Goldblatt, Daniel Fitzpatrick, Robert H.
MacCandless, James R. Mageean, P. Joseph Tomelty, John O'Malley, and John
J. Moss hereby mutually agree to become partners in the business of the
production and presentation of plays and other entertainments of a like
nature for the period and on the terms hereinafter expressed that is to say:-

1.   The partnership shall be deemed to have commenced on the 1st day of
September 1942 and shall be terminated by mutual arrangement only.

2.   Any partner may at the end of the first or any subsequent year of the
partnership retire from the partnership on giving not less than six calendar
months' previous notice in writing to the other partners or partner or
leaving the same at the place of business of the partnership and at the
expiration of such year the partnership shall determine accordingly as to the
partner giving or leaving such notice and thereupon the provisions of clauses
2A, 2B and 2C of these presents shall (with the substitution of the continuing
partners or partner for the surviving partners or partner and of the retiring
partner for the representatives of the deceased partner and other conse-
quential modifications) apply as if the retiring partner had died at the
expiration of such year. The retiring partner in the event of the purchase
of his share under the said provisions shall not for 10 years from the date
of his retirement directly or indirectly carry on or be concerned or
interested in the business of the production and presentation of plays and
other entertainments of a like nature as principal agent manager artist or
servant within 50 miles from the then principal place of business of the
partnership.

3.   The death or retirement of any partner shall not dissolve the partnership
as to the other partners.

4.   The style or firm of the partnership shall be Ulster Group Theatre.

5.   Subject to the provisions of these presents the partners shall be
entitled to the capital and property for the time being of the
partnership and to the goodwill of the business in the following shares, that
is to say, the said Harold Goldblatt shall be entitled to forty per cent
thereof and the other named partners shall each be entitled to ten per cent
thereof.

6.   The capital of the partnership shall be the sum of £500 to be contributed
by the partners in the shares in which they are hereinbefore declared to be
entitled to the capital and property of the partnership.

7.   If any further capital shall be at any time or times be considered by the
partners to be necessary or expedient for efficiently carrying on the
business the same shall be contributed by the partners in the shares in
which they are for the time being entitled to the existing capital of the
partnership.

Contract for the founding of the Group.

Joe with Sybil Thorndyke, other actress unknown.

The McCooeys *at home, left to right, J.G. Devlin, Min Milligan, John McBride and Mina Dornan.*

Joe, Jean Reid, Gavin Stewart, Margaret D'Arcy, Daphne May, Alfred Arnold, James Boyce, Harold Goldblatt, Robert Dempster and (Min Milligan). Possibly the cast outside Liverpool Playhouse.

With Harold Goldblatt and Hilton Edwards at the Group.

Min Milligan in the film Irish Interlude, *early 50s. Her apron is still worn onstage.*

At BBC.

Sam Thompson in production of Joseph Tomelty's All Souls' Night.

Min and Bobby Loughan in Barnum was Right *or* Mugs and Money. *Bobby was his favourite Willie John.*

ALHAMBRA BRADFORD
Telephone: 27001

Managing Director: Gwladys Laidler Woodhead, M.B.E.
Director and Secretary: Rowland Hill   Manager: George Baines

FOR ONE WEEK commencing MONDAY, 1st JUNE

EVENINGS (Monday to Friday) at 7.30   SATURDAY (Two performances) at 5 and 8 p.m.

PRICES OF ADMISSION.   Stalls: 8/6, 7/-, 5/6 ;   Circle: 7/6 ;   Balcony: 3/6

Box Office open daily 9.30 a.m. to 7.30 p.m.

Taurus Presentations

in association with James Whiteley Limited

present

ANNA NEAGLE

in

A New Experience in Suspense

PERSON UNKNOWN

**A thriller by David Butler
from an original play by Olive
Chase and Stanley Clayton**

DIRECTED BY JOHN BARRON

with

**PHILIP
LATHAM**

**JOHN
ALDERTON**

**JOSEPH
TOMELTY**

and co-starring
by arrangement with M.G.M.

and **JENNIFER WOOD**

CHARLES TINGWELL

as Inspector Conway

Alhambra, Bradford poster.

Rowel Friers (1948) s ketch - Drawn from the stalls in the Group. Joe as Lemmie in Of Mice and Men.

May 27th 1945.

Joseph Tomelty, Esq.
Belfast.

tingrith
station road totnes devon
totnes 2359

Dear Mr Tomelty,

You frighten me when you say you will amend your play on the lines suggested by me. Don't. There is no more thankless job than to alter one's play at another's suggestion. I did it twice at the advice of others — "Crimson in the Tricolour" & "Frost in the Flower" never again.

You must work everything out your own way. We learn through blundering. My way is my own way; yours, yours. If I were to advise you at all, I'd say write a new play, & when you've done that — after a year or so, read the play you are thinking of or writing, & see then what you think of it. Thanks for reference to "Juno." I'm glad it was a success. I knew Carl Clopet was to produce it — for two weeks, he said. I haven't heard from him since its production. All the best.

Sean O'Casey

Letter from Sean O'Casey.

At Retreat at Mount Mellary after the accident in 1956.

On Tour with Anna Neagle and Charles Tingwell in Persons Unknown.

Lena and Joe with Frances in 'Patricia Mulholland' dancing costume.

Plaque unvieling at 22, The Shore. Left to Right, Hannah, Colin, Ruth Carnegie, Roma, Joe Sumner, the Mayor of Newtownards David Smith, Kate Sumner and Frances.

17

The Accident and Afterwards

A FTER THE SUCCESS OF TOMELTY'S performance in *The Passing Day* and the memory of his contribution to *Odd Man Out*, a new career in film beckoned. He acquired, in Freddie Joachim, an agent, soon a personal friend, who was assiduous in finding him character parts. As often happened to beginners at the time, his first appearance (apart from 'Gin Jimmy') in the film *Treasure Hunt* (1952), was uncredited, but cast as 'Will Sparks' in David Lean's *The Sound Barrier* (1952), he showed that he was a natural for the screen – in the popular phrase, 'The camera loved him.' The plot concerned the problems facing pilots in jet aircraft that can go faster than the speed of sound. It was the first of several films in which he played 'helpful old codgers' of various stripes. It was something of a generalisation for he was nothing if not versatile. Will Sparks was a genius with a slide rule, the engineer's best tool in pre-chip days, and the vibrancy of his performance is still palpable.

In *The Gentle Gunman* (1952), he plays 'Dr Brannigan' who,

sympathetic to the IRA's aims if not their methods, engages in debate with the Englishman Henry Truethome (played by Gilbert Harding) about those ideals. Harding was then the most iconic figure on British television and usually played himself with little attempt at special characterisation. Another fine film in which Tomelty played an important part was *Meet Mr Lucifer* (1953). An Ealing comedy, it represented a fairly weak cinematic response to the threat of universal television. Stanley Holloway, who played Mr Lucifer, was pleased to use the box as a source of diabolical trouble, causing dissension among families and general dysfunction in society. Tomelty was Mr Pedelty, an accountant with a firm who is given early retirement because he is to be replaced by a machine. In one brilliant scene he demonstrates that, using an abacus, he is the match for any calculating machine. The retirement gift of a television set he accepts and soon becomes the most popular man in the street but realises almost too late what the thing is doing to his life. It was a part that suited him perhaps better than any except 'Gin' Jimmy or Will Sparks.

In *Hell Below Zero* (1954), a film about the crew of a whaling ship, the *Kista Dan*, with Hollywood star Alan Ladd (1913–64) in the lead, Tomelty played McPhee, the captain of the whaler. He was then only forty-three, but with his shock of bushy white hair and make-up he could look older. Ladd was very anxious about some of the scenes in which they both had to appear, in case 'the old guy' should have a mishap, not realising that 'the old guy' was only two years his senior. They, of course, became good friends and Ladd arranged for a trip for the two of them to Paris. Unfortunately Mark Robson, the director, forbade Tomelty to leave London where the studio scenes were being shot: 'Joe ain't going out of London – I want Joe in the can for Monday.' (In fact, as we have seen, he had to play truant that weekend for cogent reasons to do with *The McCooeys*.) The effect on his family of his having to grow a beard for the part of Jim Heeler in David Lean's *Hobson's Choice* (1954) has already been described. The daughters especially were dismayed, to say the least of it, at their father's pied appearance, hairy in white, black and red.

Then came *Bhowani Junction* (1956). The film was based on a novel by John Masters (1914–83) about the social chaos at the time of the declaration of Indian independence from Britain in 1947; the director was the famous George Cukor (1899–1983). The chief character is Victoria Jones, the Anglo-Indian daughter of a railway worker, also Eurasian, who, having served as a nurse in the British army during the war, now is torn apart by conflicting loyalties. It was a starring part for Ava Gardner, then at her stellar zenith. The part of her father, the train driver, was played by Tomelty, and other leading roles by Stewart Granger (1913–93) and Bill Travers (1922–94). The part of Ghan Shyam (aka 'Davey'), the communist agitator, was played by Tomelty's close friend, the Austrian actor, Peter Illing.

Location scenes were shot in Lahore, in eastern Pakistan, and while there, Tomelty made the passing acquaintance of Justice Kenneth – afterwards Baron – Diplock (1907–85) who gave his name to the juryless Diplock courts that were used in political cases during the Northern Ireland troubles. Diplock and his wife were in Lahore and visited the set, and afterwards, while they were sitting drinking, Mrs Diplock's cardigan slipped off the back of her chair. Tomelty rose to fetch it but, as he later described it, she waved him away and clapped her hands together to bring a Pakistani waiter to do the job instead. By one of those ironies of fate they were destined to meet again in an equally uncomfortable situation.

The studio interior scenes were shot at the Metro-Goldwyn-Mayer studios at Elstree Studios, Borehamwood, beginning on 11 April 1955 and on the 30th, Tomelty, though on standby, was not required for shooting. He was staying at a small private hotel called the Grosvenor Restaurant, owned by Charles Wolfram. Characteristically they became very friendly. Wolfram had to collect his five-year-old daughter, Margaret, and her friend, Angela

O'Farrell, from school and asked Tomelty to come along for the ride. On the way home with Tomelty in the front seat, Wolfram drove through a red light at a crossroads at Bushey Heath, hitting another car driven by Douglas Robinson of Hendon Way, London. The occupants were taken to the Watford Peace Memorial Hospital and the children later transferred to the children's ward of Shrodell's Hospital in Watford. The three adults all had head injuries, but Tomelty's condition, having crashed through the windscreen and hit a tree with his head, was labelled 'most serious'. The children soon recovered as did Wolfram and the other driver.

That afternoon, about four o'clock, Frances, who was eight, was having a dolls' tea-party in the hallway with real Jacob's Mikado biscuits. A few schoolfriends helped with the ceremony. Roma, who was ten, was in the living-room while Lena was in the kitchen, ironing. The phone rang and Lena picked it up, smiling when she heard Freddie's voice but when Roma heard her say, 'Is he hurt?' and her mother begin to cry, she knew that something terrible had happened. Lena told her to run as quickly as she could to McGowans' to tell Josie that her father had had an accident. She had to get to Nutts Corner airport and would Gerry bring the car? She also asked everybody to pray for him. Roma ran up Stockman's Lane and across the Andersonstown Road into Dunmisk Park and was pleased to find Gerry at home. Josie McGowan and her cousin Eilish O'Boyle, who was a Dominican nun, Sr Xaviera, were in the house as well. While Gerry got the car ready, the nun took Roma's hand and assured her: 'You know, Rosemary, God is very good.' Gerry and Josie, who had been old neighbours in Stockman's Lane, took Lena to the airport where, as Freddie had advised, a seat had been booked for her on the London plane. MGM had been in touch with British European Airways and would hold the aircraft until Gerry could get her there.

The Watford Peace had not the facility for the brain surgery that would have been immediately done in a larger hospital, a fact that proved ironically to be a lifesaver. J.A.E. O'Connell, a leading neurosurgeon under whose care Tomelty was later placed, said that the trauma of an operation after the shock of the accident would have been fatal. As Lena sat by his bed, he briefly swam into consciousness to ask: 'Are the children all right?' and 'Are you all right for money?' and then lapsed into a coma that lasted for six weeks. The story was big, not only in Ireland but internationally, with daily bulletins about his more or less static condition. Letters began to arrive from all over the world, some addressed to 'Joe Tomelty, Belfast'. Wherever there was an Irish community, wherever green was worn, expatriates wrote letters of sympathy, solidarity and the assurance of prayers. Nuns, brothers and priests sent blue aerogrammes from Africa, America, India and Oceania. Telegrams came from Dirk Bogarde, Laurence Olivier, Douglas Fairbanks Jnr, and a bouquet of flowers arrived with a message from Ava Gardner, his screen daughter: 'Pater, darling, hurry up and get well!'

After six weeks Tomelty began to rally, coming slowly out of his comatose state. It was reckoned then that his mental age was that of his daughter Roma. His appearance was startling; the trademark mane of white hair was gone, shaved to determine the nature of his lesions, but his hair, cropped to the skull, was beginning to grow again. His beard was extensive after six weeks of growth, because his mouth had been injured and it would have caused him too much pain to shave it. The girls had been told that their father was ill, which they assumed was something like flu or measles. They had prepared a welcome-home banner but he scarcely seemed to notice it. Now with cropped skull and a bushy beard that was black, grey and the Tomelty family red, he seemed a stranger to the girls. They ran forward expecting the usual bear hugs but as he came up the steps he shook their hands instead. In spite of the anticipated difficulties and many others that soon manifested themselves, Lena decided that the summer of 1955 – and an especially glorious summer it was – would be spent in Carnlough as usual. Everyone sought an acceptable normality and it was probably the correct decision though it meant an intolerable strain on Lena, her mother and the faithful Ma Ritchie.

Lily Ritchie had joined the family circle as a home help, with the eventual blessing of the paterfamilias who 'wanted no strangers about the house'. He relented when the wife of John Ritchie, a friend from Portaferry, now living in Beechmount, off the Falls Road, a Scotswoman who had been 'in service' in the days of cooks and parlourmaids, agreed to come to work for the Tomeltys. She signed herself 'MA Ritchie' on Christmas and birthday cards but was always 'the Ma' to all the family. John, her husband, died of tuberculosis and she came to help in the bungalow. She was a well-established, if intermittent, member of the ménage long before the accident and it was she and Granny Minnie who looked after the girls while Lena sat in the hospital in St Albans, to which her husband had been moved. They considered her 'frugal', though that was not the word they used. Not one for extra biscuits, she would compromise with 'We'll break this one in half!' The Tomelty children were not spoilt even before the accident, no matter what their envious schoolmates might suppose. Lena and their father had tough working-class rearing and though they loved their girls, it would never have occurred to them to indulge them. After the accident everything had to change.

'The Ma' was a prodigious worker, strong and willing. The medical experts had suggested, as part of a painfully slow rehabilitation, that a move to a bigger house with high ceilings might be advisable, so they crossed the road from the modern bungalow to an old Victorian mansion, spacious but damnably hard to heat. The day they moved, the girls were in awe at the sight of 'the Ma' carrying unaided across Stockman's Lane a whole wardrobe. She had been a weekly visitor but when Lena went to London to spend weekends with her husband or went to Paris during the filming of *John and Julie* (1955), she and her daughter

Eileen stayed with the children. The children suggested that for everyone's convenience, 'the Ma' should move into the garage; it struck them as a perfectly reasonable solution to the accommodation question. She also stayed during the six weeks of waiting after the accident and went with them to Carnlough in June. While she was in residence in the bungalow, an eccentric neighbour, Mrs Jenkins, called with a message for 'Mrs Tomelty'. She claimed to be clairvoyant and found divination in the crystal ball. She knew about the accident – the whole city knew about it – but she had cast Tomelty's horoscope and she had discovered that he would be home again in early July. It was bad theatre but on 8 July he was at the front door.

The survival had defied all predictions; there was a long convalescence and recovery was far from total. The work of rehabilitation begun in England by O'Connell had painfully to be continued by Lena. When Tomelty landed in Carnlough, he moved as if by instinct to a captain's chair at the head of the table in the kitchen and, as it seemed to the observant Roma, he was there all that summer. O'Connell had warned that inertia, however restful, was not an option. He said to Lena and she often quoted it as a kind of mantra: 'If you want your husband to sit forever in the corner, then so be it! Otherwise you must take him out, however much distress this will at times cause.' He insisted that if Tomelty was ever to reach a level of normality he must go into society, be part of his accustomed world, no matter how difficult that might be to implement. This was Lena's main reason for keeping their usual holiday date in Carnlough, intolerably stressful as it proved.

One aspect of the summer was the constant stream of visitors, almost as O'Connell prescribed, but they had to be entertained to the kind of formal meal that a hotel might supply, like cooked ham and salad. There was no china, nor matching cutlery, no wine glasses for the Beaujolais that was Tomelty's favourite tipple – and no convenient means of getting supplies of it. In the weeks that followed, the sieve of time separated the true friends from the hangers-on and those merely clients. David Kennedy and his wife Maddie, J.J. (Seamus) Campbell and Josie, Sam and Mildred Bell, John and Elizabeth Boyd, Dr Jim Ryan and Harry Gibson stayed faithful. A local man, Paddy Connolly, often took Tomelty and the family for a drive. This kindness was hugely important to them at the time. The family felt, with some justification, that some of Tomelty's colleagues in the Group showed little charity or real concern. They had lost a valuable source of employment and profit – no more long runs at the Minor Hall, no more *McCooeys* scripts or challenging radio plays. The party was over and the hangers-on had left. Later, as his condition, physical and mental, improved, he was able to renew acquaintance with old friends: Sam Thompson, who arranged for a part for him in *Over the Bridge* (1960) and his wife May; Jimmy Vitty of the Linen Hall Library; the artists Willie Conor, Rowel Friers, Paddy Woods; the journalist James Kelly and other members of the Ten Club that met at the Chalet D'Or in Fountain Street.

Other friends presented themselves. One was Jim Eccles who worked for Baird's Motors. Earlier in the year Tomelty had taken delivery of a Sunbeam Talbot and had driven it to Nutts Corner, then the Belfast airport. There was a publicity still taken, and after Tomelty went back to the filming of *Bhowani Junction*, Eccles stored the car. He was at the airport with the car when Tomelty arrived back on his release from hospital but realised that he could not possibly drive. It was Eccles who had continually to devise reasons why Tomelty could not be given the car when he regularly arrived at the showrooms demanding his Sunbeam Talbot.

The holiday of 1955, Roma and Frances also remember as the Lemon Barley Water summer. During her hospital vigil Lena stayed at a B&B in St Albans run by a Mrs Gladys Dutton who made wonderful Lemon Barley Water, then something of a luxury. As Tomelty recovered in the hospital, he was able to drink it and

Mrs Dutton passed on the secret recipe. It was made in copious quantities that summer and it is still a nudge-worthy event when the sisters are offered it.

The most obvious change that the children noticed in their father was an obsession with waste – a kind of recessional legacy from the poverty of his childhood. To ease overcrowding, especially at the start of the sojourn in Carnlough when so many visitors came, Roma and Frances took their meals on the wonky table in the parlour, fighting about who should have the blistered part. If they left any food, he would become angry, which was not recommended medically because of the danger of fitting. Here 'the Ma' again came to the rescue smuggling leftovers – chop bones, pieces of fat, the usual debris that even adults won't face – in her apron pockets. Tomelty's emotions at this time were very near the surface and at times he could not control laughter or rage. Lena bore the brunt heroically and by dint of selfless service and management skills gradually won him back to a remarkable level of normality. He could still act, especially in film or television, where short takes allowed him to memorise sufficiently the dialogue. He was able to appear successfully as Aneas in a 1971 television production of his moving play about gentle madness, *The Singing Bird* (1948), but it took him some time to get into the part of Davy Mitchell in *Over the Bridge*, though the play was so strong and so well acted that it did not matter.

In a schools' programme broadcast in the early 1970s, he played John Quinn in the scene from *All Souls' Night* (1948) in which Molly Trainor teaches the illiterate Quinn the magic, as it seems to him, of being able to read: 'And that's a nought. Round like a sail ring or the eye of a herrin'.' I happened to hear it and was struck by its brilliance. I afterwards learnt from one of the production team that it had been done in a single take, the very first. As the months went by, Tomelty became more like his old self, perfectly capable of rational conversation but ever conscious of the writing skill he knew he had lost. He frequently said that he thanked God for what he had been given and what had been taken away. His agent Freddie was tireless in persuading film companies to give him parts, often putting his own reputation on the line until Tomelty retired after *The Black Torment* (1964), a horror film set in eighteenth-century England in which he played Sir Giles Fordyke, who, because of a stroke, is able to communicate only by signs and cannot reveal the awful family secret.

The move across the road meant that he could concentrate on the garden and a new hobby, not always successful, the making of home-made wine. He would use anything from the hedgerows capable of being rendered safely into liquor. At the back of the house in Stockman's Lane was an old washhouse with two large sinks and this was the vinery. The children called it 'Frankenstein's Laboratory', where bubbling and fermenting was constant and explosions not unknown. His patent elderberry taken hot was a specific for curing colds overnight and on frequent journeys into the country he would collect fruit wherever it grew wild. He was especially attracted to the vegetation round ruined cottages, claiming that elderberries were grown there once on a day as a panacea. On one occasion, as he prepared to share a home vintage with an actor called Bobby Loughan, who had been a hit as Willie John in the Dublin productions of the *Barnums*, the bottle exploded all over the actor's impeccable grey suit and matching suede shoes, turning all into purple. For a man with the normal store of impatience, especially when driving, he was remarkably careful with the fruit during the preparation.

He also started gardening. At the start his tomatoes did not always do well. When Alan Whitsitt interviewed him in October 1974, he was invited out to the conservatory to take some, but as he wrote: 'A literary genius yes, but the world's worst tomato grower I observed as he tried his best to fill a bowl with his crop, each no larger than a gooseberry. "They'll make a nice chutney," he apologised with a wink.' Maybe it was the wrong season; certainly when he moved to Blackrock in 1977, tomatoes and wine played a continuing part in his life. When Roma wrote a sketch of his life for an early 1990s but otherwise undated supplement to the *Honest Ulsterman*, her concluding sentence reads: 'He now lives quietly with his wife in Blackrock, County Louth, and arguably grows the best tomatoes in the world.'

Robert Hogan (1930–99) is well known as the indefatigable chronicler of Irish literature, with such magisterial publications as the two-volume *Dictionary of Irish Literature* (1996) and *After the Irish Renaissance* (1968), a detailed history of Irish drama 'since *The Plough and the Stars*'. In the latter book he describes a visit paid to Tomelty in Stockman's Lane. He found 'a heavyish man with a superb actor's face, a mane of thick white hair' who 'lives in a sprawling, comfortable old house with a large garden on the outskirts of Belfast':

> He is an actor in his conversation – volatile, alive, full of anecdote, and always about to jump up and act out a scene or illustrate a point. He sums up his work by saying that his comedies are local and have no universal content, and that his serious plays are not good enough.

I quote this not to indicate agreement with Tomelty's dismissal of his own work, but to establish that within a decade of the catastrophe he was coherent, critical and showing no signs of serious dysfunction. His own will and the continuous care of his wife had made him whole again or nearly so.

By the time of the accident, Tomelty was one of the most identifiable people in Belfast. Those who did not know him to speak to knew who he was and if they did attempt to strike up a conversation with him they were met with great geniality and an Ancient Mariner reluctance to part. This was true in all parts of the sectarian city because he seemed to bestride its narrow world. His memory stayed with the people about whom he wrote so lovingly and so cleverly in *The McCooeys* and it lasted for his lifetime, even though he lived for part of his later life in County

Louth. At the gala reopening of the Grand Opera House in 1980, Anne Milligan, Tomelty's niece, arrived at the portable barricade that surrounded any building which in those years the Northern Ireland Secretary, Humphrey Atkins (1922–96), was visiting. She asked one of the policemen on duty when the show would be over, explaining that she was there to pick up Joe Tomelty. The man grinned broadly, said 'Bobby Greer: schlup up yer schloup,' and removed the barrier to allow her to wait inside the safety zone. After nearly thirty years of *McCooey* silence it was quite an accolade.

Because of his friendliness, his capacity for entertaining the interviewer and the rich store of anecdotes and memories he could summon from the vasty deep of his past, Tomelty was in regular demand for interviews for newspaper, radio and television. On 5 October 1956, a year and a half after the accident, he was profiled for the *Belfast Telegraph* by Martin Wallace who described how 'ideas are spinning in his head but he is not yet able to give writing the concentration it needs. The ideas are there ... but they need to be disciplined.' The dysfunction that prevented that concentration persisted and, though tolerably happy, he really knew that the high fantastical line which, begun with *April in Assagh* (1953), seemed to him to be the future pattern for his plays, would not now be developed.

Life was not all grim, however, even in the early days. His friend J.J. Campbell (1910–79), known to close friends as Seamus, whose damning exposé of Ulster sectarianism in *Orange Terror* Tomelty greatly admired, was then head of education in St Joseph's College of Education and an active member of the senate of the Queen's University of Belfast (QUB) who proposed his name as recipient of a Master of Arts degree (*honoris causa*) in 1956. It was a daring thing for a sober institution like QUB to recognise an actor as worthy of the honour but then he was a very special actor, as well as playwright. The citation reproduced below by permission of the *Annual Record of the Queen's Association*

1956 was delivered by Professor L.M. Gonzalez-Llubera, Dean of the Faculty of Art:

> The name of Joseph Tomelty evokes in Ulster listeners a feeling of gratitude, that immediate response that the born dramatist and man of theatre in close contact with the country of his birth first seeks and then successfully awakens in his public.
>
> The stage has been Tomelty's constant passion, and his early environment, the fishing folk of Portaferry, the toil of Belfast's major industry, the substance and inspiration of his work.
>
> This and much more lives again in his plays, notably *All Souls' Night* and *Is the Priest at Home?* And others, all immediately popular successes – in which no less than in his novels his life's experience is powerfully expressed, and his gift of observation and characterisation fully displayed.
>
> As actor, playwright and business manager he was identified with Ulster Group Theatre from its earliest days. He was its guiding spirit over a number of years, until the inevitable London adventure with the Northern Ireland Festival of Britain Theatrical Company and the beginnings of his career in films and later television.
>
> Lastly there are his numerous broadcast scripts. He is the creator of the radio serial whose characters are household words, in Ulster and wherever Ulster people are.
>
> The man who represents so well in his work and in his life the native genius of this Province also belongs to its University. We shall be glad to count him among our graduates.

Such recognition came at a very delicate period in his convalescence and it was undoubtedly therapeutic.

In all, Tomelty made twenty-nine films, some excellent, some decidedly run-of-the-mill. In all of them he gave interesting performances, doing unconsciously what in the theatre is called 'up-staging' – perhaps in films it should be 'up-setting' – in both senses. A number made before the accident were released afterwards, including *John and Julie* (1955), about two children who run away to London to see the coronation of Elizabeth II;

Simba (1955), about the Mau Mau rising in Kenya in which he played a doctor again; *Bedevilled* (1955), about a clerical student who protects a murder suspect, with Tomelty ideally cast as Fr Cunningham, and *A Prize of Gold* (1955), about bullion smuggling in occupied Berlin just after the war, in which he had the appropriately avuncular role of Uncle Dan. When these appeared, filmgoers thought that his recovery was complete. He did find some further parts after the crash because of his reputation as an actor and the reassurance of Freddie Joachim. These included the parts of Detective Inspector Cleary in *Timeslip* (1955), Peter Coffin, the inn-keeper, in *Moby Dick* (1956) and Dr William O'Loughlin, the liner's surgeon in *A Night to Remember* (1958), about the sinking of the *Titanic*. He also appeared in seven television dramas including a memorable performance as Michael James, the father of Pegeen Mike, in Synge's *The Playboy of the Western World*. Eventually he found the physical demands of film work increasingly difficult but there is no doubt that these immediately post-accident jobs and the accolade from Queen's helped with the long time healing.

Less welcome was the attitude of the judge at the compensation hearing, who by ill-chance was Kenneth Diplock, Tomelty's old acquaintance from Lahore. The award by the High Court against Wolfram, who drove the car, of £17,500, was grossly inadequate, especially when one considers that Tomelty was virtually unable to work at his profession for the last forty years of his life. The family are convinced that Diplock's peroration influenced the jury to award lesser damages than they might have done with a different president. The judgement is quoted in an account of an interview with Tomelty written by Alan Whitsitt in the *Belfast News Letter* on 14 October 1974:

> I hope he will forgive me if I say that having seen him in the witness box, I think it impossible for a man of his talent and temperament not to give a superb performance of a man suffering from very severe head injuries.

> But it was a performance which I think was much larger than
> life. I don't suggest for a moment that there was any conscious
> exaggeration in his evidence but I think he found it impossible
> not to live the part he was playing.

A horrified silence seems to me the only response to such
remarks, now fifty-five years after their being uttered. Tomelty
was not in court to hear them – in fact he never remembered any
detail of what happened that day after being driven in the car and
waking up in hospital with a fractured skull, but all the expert
medical evidence made it clear that his condition was no act.

That piece includes Tomelty's own account of his condition at
age sixty-two, nearly twenty years after the occurrence. It took
place at the height of the Troubles when Stockman's Lane had
'been turned into a cul-de-sac by military barriers and dragon's
teeth'. Access to 217 was awkward but Tomelty seemed
unperturbed as he stroked Nisha, his Siamese cat, and talked about
'his past, the present and the future'. The conversation ranged
about the whole of his impressive career: 'Writing and playing for
radio is what I enjoyed most out of life.' He agreed that he would
be most widely remembered for his work with *The McCooeys*, '
a fictitious name that I made up for neutrality's sake'. With a
certain amount of heroic patience he claimed that there were many
who said he was never the same after the accident, 'but considered
what change there was, was for the better'. He was 'resting', he
said, rather than retired but the word was inappropriate for a man
with so active and creative a mind, buzzing with ideas for new
plays, treasured lines of dialogue, the possibility of writing a play
that would have *The McCooeys* facing the Troubles.

Whitsitt and his subject had by this stage moved out to view
his famous tomato crop. As the conversation returned to more
serious subjects, Tomelty agreed that 1955 was the worst year of
his life and thought when asked that the best might have been
1951, the year of *The Passing Day* and the beginning of his film
career. The *News Letter* piece was one of a series with the general

title of *1951 ... It Was Their Year* and it gave Whitsitt an ideal
opportunity to record the excellent witty conversation of his
subject. He told of his struggle to excise stage-Irish expressions
from his film dialogue. He refused to say the line: 'I'll be after
having a drink.' And won the battle. He also eventually was
granted the privilege due to a man who was writer, as well as actor,
of improving by ad-libbing his given script.

Two years later he was interviewed by Billy Simpson for the
Belfast Telegraph on his sixty-fifth birthday and returned to the
theme of national dramatic stereotyping:

> There are three people I've yet to meet: a Scotsman who says,
> 'Hoots, mon, ah dinna ken'; a Welshman who says, 'Indeed to
> my goodness' – and an Irishman who says 'Bejabers, what are
> you after havin'?'

To both these interviewers he tried to explain the lethargy. To
Simpson:

> I can't settle to write any more. The typewriter stands there and
> I can't even take the top off it. I'm not physically lazy. I walk
> three miles into town every day. It's mentally. My telegraphic
> address should be 'Manana'. Tomorrow. Always tomorrow! ...
> I'm an absent-minded professor these days.

To Whitsitt: 'I've got this great idea for a play right now ... but
people might be bored by it for it's about the Troubles and we've
had more than enough of that.' He also described another
successful crusade for realism in broadcast dialogue:

> It was he [Larry Morrow] who helped me break down an age-
> old rule in the BBC that banned four-letter words. Harmless
> ones by today's standards, of course, but they nevertheless
> insisted on changing my Damns into Dangs and in one play I
> wrote I had included four of these. I kicked up a stink and Larry
> backed me up. And a 'shocked' radio audience heard the word
> 'damn' for the first time.

In yet another interview for the *News Letter* given to Mervin Pauley in the series *Pauley's People: Mervyn Pauley Talks to People who Matter in Ulster*, Tomelty conveyed one last typical memory of his campaign for realistic dialogue: 'When people thinking it's the way people talk greet me with "The top o' the mornin' to you", I tell them, "And the arse of the evening to you."'

18
Going South

AS THE NORTHERN IRELAND TROUBLES GREW more intense and the girls went away to pursue their careers in theatre, the parents began to consider moving house. The large Victorian mansion had been recommended by doctors and psychiatrists as a therapeutic option for the patient. Tomelty had had space to develop his wine-making hobby and the gardens were extensive. The large rooms with their high ceilings, however, were harder to heat and now the place was too big for just the two of them. Weeping gelignite was dumped in a neighbour's garden and, living where they did, they felt that the ordinary business of living had become fraught with, it seemed, never-ending tension. Reluctantly they decided to move away from the troubled city. Not that Tomelty had any fear of either side; any man who could make his way into a florist's on the Protestant Shankill Road to order Orange lilies would not have been put off by the threat of bomb or bullet.

In the autumn of 1977 they decided it was time to go south, if only temporarily. Lena always said that she wanted to come home to die 'under the Black Mountain'. Leaving any house is copybook stressful but with a large mansion like No 217, occupied in illness and recovered health for twenty years, was fraught. Much accumulated debris had to be disposed of, including 150 copies of an extreme paper, a forerunner of the *Protestant Telegraph*. Also disposed of were many memorabilia of a multi-faceted talent, including the hundreds of telegrams, cards and letters delivered to the hospitals in Watford and St Albans. Lena's niece Anne had a cottage in Carlingford, County Louth; the Drumgooles lived in Dundalk; Therese Coey, the soprano star of many musical evenings, was a regular visitor to the county, as was Molly Bonner of the Genesian Players, who staged the first production of *The End House* outside the Abbey. They found a bungalow in Blackrock, a seaside resort, four miles southeast of Dundalk on the tidal sandy Dundalk Bay. There was a garden and a greenhouse for the tomatoes and the sea was close by.

In the interview in *Pauley's People* it is clear that Tomelty regarded his hegira as a watershed and he was meditative, philosophical and reminiscent as he talked and his memories of the Belfast of his youth and young manhood – he was only twelve when he came to live there – were close to the surface:

> When I came here first you could get a pint of White Cross for a
> tanner [six old pence], a pie for fourpence, into the Alhambra
> [the music-hall turned cinema in North Street that was allowed
> to keep its liquor licence] for another tanner and still have enough
> for the fare home. Ah the old Alhambra, where the drunks at the
> bar at the back used to roll their empties down the central aisle,
> especially if the show wasn't up to scratch.

Like many another sixty-six-year-old he felt that the old atmosphere was gone, not just that sectarian attitudes had hardened, but that the overheard remarks from the street characters that he collected to use in his work seemed to have dried up. As he recalled: 'One compliment people paid me when I was writing *The McCooeys* was that they didn't know which side we were on.' One of his obvious gifts as a writer was his intimate knowledge of ordinary people, whether city-dwellers or the often guyed 'culchies'. He believed that the Northern Catholic had more in common with the Northern Protestant than with the Southern Catholic even before the fifty years of partition, but he deplored the tribal hatred that blighted the province where true Irish hospitality lived – even if delivered without frills. As he once wrote: 'The Irish Catholic is too busy listening for the sound of Gabriel's trumpet; the Irish Protestant has not cleared his ears of Knox's thundering.' An inevitable sadness crept into his voice when he told Pauley: 'A psychiatrist told me that the sort of accident I had would mean I probably wouldn't be able to read or write. I still can't get into reading and the accident was the reason I did not start writing again.' Typically he cheered up again, remarking that he had always loved living near the sea, being born and bred in Portaferry. 'I'll still be able to look out and see the Mournes in the distance.'

He and Lena lived in Louth until the late 1980s. While there, a journalist from the *Dundalk Democrat* paid him a visit in June 1983, printing an unsigned interview on 2 July 1983, shortly after the reprint by Blackstaff Press in Belfast of *The Apprentice*. It gave Tomelty an opportunity to rehearse again some early memories. He recalled missing an English class in the College of Technology when he was twelve because there was a film he wanted to see. 'I knew I had to have a good excuse so I had to say my grandmother died. I ended up being complimented because in those days everyone took two days off and I only took one.' An essay he wrote on 'Trees' was read out at the class he missed and the next day, the teacher, a man called Tipping, advised him to become a writer. When he admitted that he knew very few big words, the teacher told him that George Bernard Shaw, then at the height of his fame as a thinker and playwright, had a very small vocabulary. Tomelty remembered a time in his boyhood when he found he was able to replicate the sound of a fife heard on a neighbour's wind-up gramophone and suggested that his interest and ability in acting stemmed from then. A production of *Juno and the Paycock* (1924), done by the Abbey Players in Belfast, showed an alternative to the drawing-room, French-windows fare offered by visiting companies in the Grand Opera House. When Captain Boyle asked in Act III: 'Is there e'er a bottle of stout in the house?' it startled him and made him realise that the theatre could be about 'real' people.

As the Tomeltys grew older they started hankering for 'home' again, especially Lena who missed her native city. They had made occasional visits – it was only fifty-one miles from Dundalk to Belfast and there was an excellent train service. They kept a professional and parental eye on the theatrical careers of their daughters, and from time to time the prospect of crack in the Chalet D'Or and around the special table drew Tomelty back to the Red-Brick City, as his friend Denis Ireland (1894–1974) called it. Roma found them a little place near Fruithill Park behind the Falls Bowling Tennis Grounds. Benraw Green was a modern development and in it was a suitable flat. They were back where they had lived for nearly thirty years, about half a mile from Stockman's Lane. There were a few special events. In the summer of 1984, Tomelty and his friend Sam Hanna Bell were made life members of the Linen Hall Library, that, along with the Carnegie Library on the Falls Road and Campbell's Coffee House, had been his university. A bust was commissioned by the Arts Council of Northern Ireland from Carolyn Mulholland and unveiled on 1 October 1991 at their headquarters as part of his eightieth-birthday celebrations. Wife Lena, daughters Roma and Frances, son-in-law Colin Carnegie and grandchildren Rachael and Ruth were present and the unveiling ceremony was carried out by the actor, James Ellis.

Joe Tomelty died on 7 June 1995, aged eighty-four years, and after requiem mass in St Peter's Cathedral, the heart of his second homeland, was buried at Ballyphilip, Portaferry, where the story

began. A lone piper played at the funeral. The tributes saluted
him as 'the grand old man of the Ulster stage'. They noted that
there was a generation of Ulster people who would never forget
him: 'He had this extraordinary rapport with them. He loved them
and they loved him.' The *Derry Journal* of 12 June 1995 published
a valedictory item written by Fionnbarra Ó Dochartaigh with the
headline: 'Creator of *The McCooeys* laid to rest.' The success
(and the excellence) of *The McCooeys* introduced him to a much
wider public than the narrower one that knew him from the
theatre, radio drama and novels. His burgeoning film career that
ran concurrently with the radio soap made his face as well known
as his voice, usually in the frequently imitated lisp as Bobby Greer.
The schlupping-up of soup was province-wide. As Ó Dochartaigh
put it: 'It is no exaggeration to state that *The McCooeys* cleared
the streets better than a shower of rain, as even the children
gathered round the radio set to laugh, cheer or cry.' And for the
eyes of his local readers only, he also revealed that Tomelty was a
regular visitor to Derry:

> One remembers his pleasant and jovial nature, which made him
> many friends throughout the globe. He was never one to boast
> about his own talents, in fact quite the contrary, often making a
> joke at his own expense.

Lena lived on until January 2000, having spent the night of the
Millennium in hospital. She had been staying in London with
Frances and had suffered a slight stroke but was determined to
come home 'to the Black Mountain'. She died soon after, quickly
and without pain. She collapsed and said, 'Lord Jesus, help me'
and that was that. Frances was with her. She was buried from St
Matthias's, a very small church on the Glen Road. She didn't want
any singing or gifts or prayers. 'Just me and the Priest', that was
her wish. At the end of the mass the congregation said two of her
favourite prayers: *Salve Regina* and Pope Leo XIII's prayer to St
Michael the Archangel. She had always maintained that much of

the evil in the modern world was as a result of the prayer to St Michael having been removed from the Mass. She was buried with her mother Min Milligan in Milltown Cemetery.

It would be hard to over-emphasise the part she played in Tomelty's life. It was her endless wearisome care that brought the wreck of a man home and slowly helped him recover a modicum of normal health. Both were committed Catholics, she less critical of a far from flawless Church. St Peter's had been significant in both their lives; she had a fine contralto voice to match his tenor and when they returned to Belfast, she was a regular churchgoer to St Matthias's. She could be critical of priests if she felt that they were unsacerdotal. When Joe was ill at the end and the young priest arrived with Holy Communion in civvies and a bomber jacket, she was not pleased. He gradually got the message and, after a few visits, a black suit and clerical collar appeared. Soon he was practically in chasuble and stole when he came. He had taken her admonition that carrying the Blessed Sacrament, he should be appropriately dressed. She also said, more maternally than caustically, that he was a very good-looking young man and dare not run the risk of turning some young girl's head.

Tomelty, for his part, was very interested in the priestly vocation. He loved talking to priests and the daughters believed he stayed in Wynn's Hotel in Abbey Street in Dublin because it was used regularly by clergy. *Is the Priest at Home?* was written as a kind of tribute to an exacting and heroic vocation. He was as impatient as the next man when unprepared, overlong woolly sermons made Sunday Mass seem endless. He could be critical of clerical bullies and, with a wisdom he never lost, could see through the posturings of some priests unduly attracted to media exposure. He dismissed Bishop Casey as a charlatan long before there was any scandal attaching to him. A kind of impatience was, of course, symptomatic of his minor mental disarray after the accident. At a concert he abominated encores, muttering: 'Don't encourage him,' and though the family deplored it, they had to laugh when, stuck behind a slow Sunday driver on the winding roads of the Ards Peninsula, he would shout: 'Look at that! Thinks he's saving petrol! If you opened the bonnet the mother-in-law is probably in there pedalling!' His driving was safe but a little erratic, but so well known was he that though his wife referred to him as Toad of Toad Hall, any infrequent involvement with the police was kindly handled, as when once he turned into Chichester Street and went against the oncoming traffic.

Tomelty was a man of diverse talents, as writer and actor. The blow that fell when he was at the height of his powers stopped a brilliant career in a most cruel fashion but, though often wearily conscious of what he had lost, the love of family and friends and his own indomitable will made the remaining forty years full and in their own way productive. Concentrating on the disaster that befell him in mid-life, or critically decrying the remarkable achievement of *The McCooeys* as deleterious of more important work he might have achieved, is not only pointless but offensive. With more than a dozen staged plays, two remarkable novels of Ulster life, required reading for critics and historians, many highly praised if unrecorded performances in the theatre and impressive appearances in film, still happily available to us, his oeuvre remains; at least one of them, *All Souls' Night*, is an essential part of the canon of modern Irish literature. He was admired by colleagues of his own aesthetic level and is cherished even now by the few late revellers who lived for their weekly fix of Granda and Grandma McCooey, Cecil and the cleft-palated Bobby Greer, and the many other characters that gave mute Belfast a vibrant voice. His family found him wise and witty and gentle and kind both before and after the catastrophe. Enough said.

Epilogue

O N THE EXACT HUNDRETH ANNIVERSARY OF Joe Tomelty's birth, more than 150 people travelled to Portaferry to celebrate its most famous literary son. It was a spring day and the weather was, to use one of Tomelty's favourite meteorological terms, *bresk*, a word he claimed to have picked up in Ballymena. The Ulster Historical Circle (UHC) used the occasion to affix one of their blue plaques to the house on the 'Strand' where he was born and bred. The legend was the standard one:

Ulster History Circle ®
Joseph Tomelty
(1911–1995)
Author, Actor, Playwright
lived here

Among the distinguished guests were Roma and Frances, the daughters who had followed in their father's footsteps, their

children, Councillor David Smith, the mayor of Ards Borough
Council, Professor Patrick Murphy of the Heritage Literary Fund
Committee, Chris Spurr of the UHC, and Damian Smyth of the
Arts Council of Northern Ireland, who was the keynote speaker
at a tribute that also included readings from Tomelty's works and,
inevitably, music. The proceedings began with a welcome from
Sean Nolan, Secretary of the UHC, who introduced the speakers.

David Smith bade a warm welcome to all to the event with
special notice to the extended Tomelty family. Professor Murphy
praised Tomelty as a man of culture and courage, as one who had
a numinous sense of place and as a man of the people. Conscious
of his own background, his peroration neatly tied the subject into
the fuller meanings of the word 'heritage':

> If our heritage is our landscape, his writings reflect that landscape.
> If our heritage is our culture, his contribution to literature
> enhanced that culture. If our heritage is our people he portrayed
> those people for posterity. If Northern Ireland heritage is
> anything, it is embodied in Portaferry's favourite son, Joseph
> Tomelty. It is an honour for the Heritage Lottery Fund to be
> associated with his memory.

The unveiling of the plaque was performed by Roma and
Frances. This was followed by the opening of a special exhibition
in the local library about Tomelty's life and work. As Joe Sumner,
who declared it open, mused, if the amenity had existed in his
grandfather's day he would have been its most constant client.
Afterwards, in the Church of Ireland parish hall, a series of readings
from his work with linked musical events took place. Damian
Smyth, in his comprehensive and witty address, took the
opportunity to link Tomelty to the place and underscored the
effects of what he assimilated in the twelve years he spent there
on his future work, work he summarised thus:

> As an actor, playwright, novelist, short-story writer and theatre-
> manager, he achieved an enviable success, one which crossed

the borders of popular and critical acclaim and burned the image
of his rugged and sensitive features, and distinctive white hair,
across the sectarian divide into the common mythology of Belfast.

His final word of approbation was precisely appropriate: 'Well
done, Master Tomelty, scholar of your native shore.'

It was a splendid and fitting occasion; attention was finally paid
to a consummate multi-talented man. During his tribute, Smyth
quoted Willie John in *Mugs and Money*: ' ... all very Queen's
University-cum-Malachy's Old Boys'. We need not assume any
sense of inferiority on the author's part as to what the phrase might
mean to his audience. After all Tomelty also had the same
character in the same play plead for 'nice light genteel stuff. Not
ugly stuff, you know, like that fella Hanna Bell and that other
fella Tomelty writes.' He was not daunted by either establishment
figures or the lordly folk who dwell in the groves of Academe. He
knew his creative worth and the precise extent of his other talents
and would not have been put off by condescension from any
quarter. The man whose favourite dismissal phrase was: 'Pedantry
is ignorance that has read a book,' remains a triumphant figure,
secure in his place in Irish literature, who showed his greatest
courage and wry humour in the long years after a disaster that
would have felled a lesser man.

5 March 2011

About the Author

Sean McMahon was born in Derry on 18 May 1931, educated in St Columb's College, to which he returned in 1953 as a teacher of mathematics and staff member responsible for school drama. Graduated BA from Queen's University Belfast and MA (Cont Education) from University of Ulster. Reviewer of fiction, Anglo-Irish biography and literature for *Irish Press*, *Irish Independent*, *Hibernia* and *Ulster Tatler*. Contributing editor to *Éire-Ireland*, journal of the Irish America Cultural Institute, St Paul, Mi, visiting lecturer on Shakespeare to Westham House Adult College, Warwickshire. Firm believer in Dr Johnson's dictum: 'The greatest part of a writer's time is spent in reading: a man will turn over half a library to make one book.' Author of more than seventy books, one third of which are anthologies including *The Best from* The Bell, *The Derry Anthology*, *Rich and Rare*, *Taisce Duan* (with Jo O'Donoghue), *A Little Bit of Heaven*, *A Thousand Years of Dublin*, *A Thousand Years of Poetry*, *The Homes of Donegal*, *Faces of Ireland*, *Derry in Old Photographs* (both with Art Byrne) and *The Poolbeg Book of Children's Verse*. Six were collaborations, twenty-five monographs (13,000 words) on aspects of Irish biography, history and heritage, including lives of Tone, O'Connell, Emmet, Parnell, Tom Moore, books on the Irish peregrini in Europe in the first Christian millennium, the *Great Famine, the 1916 Rising, the Tan and Civil Wars, irish Mythology, Names for Children, The Claddagh Ring, The Blarney Stone, Irish Saints; Irish Insults* Dictionaries: *The Brewer's Dictionary of Irish Phrase and Fable* and *The Mercier Companion to Irish Literature* (both with Jo O'Donoghue). Compendia of short Irish biographies comprise *Lives, Great Northerners* (with Art Byrne) and *Great Irish Heroes.* Histories include *County Derry, Ulster, Ireland, Belfast, Northern Ireland, the Blitz, Battles Fought on Irish Soil* and also literary and critical biographies of Robert Lynd, and Sam Hanna Bell. Has written two adventure books for children and compiled *Shoes and Ships and Sealing-Wax* – a book of quotations for children and *The Bloody North,* an account of Ulster murders. His latest is a biography of the nationalist politician Joseph Devlin, *'Wee Joe'.*

Deeply interested in all aspects of theatre, as actor, director and writer of theatrical events. Still turning over many more than half libraries.

Select Bibliography

Works By Joseph Tomelty

Plays
The Beauty Competition (1938)
Barnum Was Right (1939)
Poor Errand (1943)
Right Again, Barnum (1943)
The End House (1944)
All Souls' Night (1948)
Down the Heather Glen (1953)
Mugs and Money (1953)
April at Assagh (1953)
The Drunken Sailor (1954)
Is the Priest at Home? (1954)

Radio
The Elopement (1939)
The Singing Bird (1948)
The McCooeys (1948–55)

Novels
Red is the Port Light (1948)
The Apprentice (1953)

Stories
'Destiny' in *Lagan* (1943)
'Confession' in *Lagan* (1944)

Films

Odd Man Out (1947)

Treasure Hunt (1952)

The Sound Barrier (1952)

You're Only Young Twice (1952)

The Gentle Gunman (1952)

The Oracle (1953)

Melba (1953)

Meet Mr Lucifer (1953)

Hell Below Zero (1954)

Hobson's Choice (1954)

Front Page Story (1954)

Happy Ever After (1954)

The Young Lovers (1954)

Devil Girl from Mars (1954)

Simba (1955)

Bedevilled (1955)

A Prize of Gold (1955)

A Kid for Two Farthings (1955)

John and Julie (1955)

Timeslip (1955)

Moby Dick (1956)

A Night to Remember (1958)

Life is a Circus (1958)

The Captain's Table (1959)

Upstairs and Downstairs (1959)

Hell is a City (1960)

The Day They Robbed the Bank of England (1960)

Lancelot and Guinevere (1963)

The Black Torment (1964)

General

Bell, Sam Hanna. *The Theatre in Ulster*. Dublin: 1972

Byrne, Ophelia. *The Stage in Ulster from the Eighteenth Century*. Belfast: 1997

—— (ed.) *State of Play: The Theatre and Cultural Identity in 20th-Century Ulster*. Belfast: 2001

Fitz-Simon, Christopher. *The Irish Theatre*. London: 1983

Hogan, Robert. *After the Irish Renaissance: A Critical History of the Irish Drama since* The Plough and the Stars. Minneapolis: 1968

Keyes, John. *Going Dark: Two Ulster Theatres*. Belfast: 2001

Odling-Smee, Hugh (ed.) *Its Own Way of Things: A Celebration of the Ulster Literary Theatre*. Belfast: 2004

Index